THE MOST
IMPORTANT CRISIS
FACING THE
21ST CENTURY

THE MOST
IMPORTANT CRISIS
FACING THE
21ST CENTURY

Arnold A. McMahon

authorHOUSE®

AuthorHouse™
1663 Liberty Drive
Bloomington, IN 47403
www.authorhouse.com
Phone: 1-800-839-8640

Published by AuthorHouse   07/26/2012

ISBN: 978-1-4772-4794-5 (sc)
ISBN: 978-1-4772-4796-9 (hc)
ISBN: 978-1-4772-4795-2 (e)

Library of Congress Control Number: 2012912794

CONTENTS

To

My first wife of 43 years, Elizabeth,
who died before her time,

My children Shiante and Edward and
daughter-in-law, Monique

My second wife, Sabrina

Their love and sense of justice has made this book possible

INTRODUCTION

The most important crisis facing the 21ˢᵗ. century is something deeper than economics, politics, war, poverty, injustice, climate change or a whole host of things. These are all affected by something much deeper. But unless we understand the fundamental cancer, we will be just putting a band-aid over these surface problems. This is not to say that each of these problems is insignificant. Indeed, they press down on humanity with a great urgency, and have always pressed down on humanity with a great urgency. Today, however, something else is in play that threatens to make these problems even more acute than before.

In the last 400 years or so, the West—and much of the rest of the world—has gone through the most significant cultural change in human history. In brief, a materialistic conception of reality has replaced one that claims there is more to reality than what we hear or see or feel or touch or taste. Not everybody, of course, accepts a materialistic conception of reality, and not everybody who does accept such a view, accepts it 100%. But it has become the dominant philosophy in much of the West, and has been seeping into the rest of the world.

Is the materialist correct? Are there any good reasons for or against it?

This book will tackle those questions, and seek to see how such a conception plays out in some of the major areas of human activity—for example, in the economy, politics, religion, love, art, education, history, science, psychology and our views on death.

I will argue that we have made a wrong turn in the road, and that this turn will eventually lead to our destruction in one form or another. The existence of nuclear weapons that can destroy planet earth 100 times over is a vivid testament to this. It is my contention that this materialistic view of reality is not only wrong, but also the root cause of much of the malaise that infects the West, whether in economics, politics, love, art—the whole gamut of human experience. Unless and until we confront this serious error, we will careen from crisis to crisis, and undermine the entire fabric of humanity's existence.

Atrocities and injustices have existed for a long time, but the current materialistic mindset undercuts and undermines one of the bulwarks against such horrors. The holocaust is but one example of that. One of mankind's central tasks has always been to treat each human being as a being of infinite worth, never merely as a means only, but always as an end in itself—as Kant would say. This is a hard and tremendous task in and of itself. The materialistic mindset makes it impossible. That is one reason why this fundamental cultural change in the last 400 years is so important—and devastating.

As I have always refrained from writing because I thought that too much was being written, a few words of explanation are now in order.

For some time as I watched crises upon crises engulf the human race, I was struck repeatedly by the superficiality of the analyses that were done on them. Whether this was due to a limited historical perspective, or to the fact that the analyzer was part of the very system that generated the crisis—or some other reason—the fact remains that I felt that none of them came to grips with the real problem.

I do not know all the answers. Nobody does. But I hope to advance the discussion in at least a small way, and help relieve a situation where an estimated 15,000 children die every day on this earth who do not have to die, where an estimated 3 billion people live on less than $2 a day—one billion of whom live in extreme poverty (which was defined by the World Bank in 2005 as living in the U.S. on $1.25 a day, buying U.S. goods)—where war is as American as apple pie, where this little piece of land called planet earth could be destroyed by humans.

Unfortunately, more has to be left out of this book than could be put in. But I will try to present some of the more important themes, and hope that others more qualified than I will expand on those and will articulate the others.

This book Is not just an intellectual exercise. It is above all a cry from a human heart, a cry for a decent, just, loving, kind world. The heartache that is caused to billions because of hunger, cruelty, greed, discrimination—and a host of other factors—is something that we feel in our own hearts. I also feel in my heart that it does not have to be this way, that there can be justice, peace, love, kindness, creativity, courage and much, much more. Humanity can be human. It is something that I will work for till my dying day. I hope that this book will advance that goal in whole or in part.

CHAPTER I

THE WEST

As the West has in significant part dominated the world militarily, politically and culturally for the past several hundred years, it might be fruitful to begin our exploration here. This is not to slight or downplay the magnificent contributions of countries such as India or China. There can be only so much on ones plate at any given moment.

The West—and much of the rest of the world—has gone through what can well be described as the greatest cultural change in history during the last 400 years or so. This change affects the very marrow of the culture, and to understand it, we must look at what went before.

For simplicity's sake, the period from approximately 400 B.C. to 1,400 A.D. can be called Culture 1. It held three fundamental beliefs.

First—and foremost—it claimed that what is truly real is not what we can see, or hear, or feel or touch or taste. What is truly real are—in Plato's terminology—the forms. They are non-spatial, non-temporal, non-physical realities which shape the world of matter. They can be perceived by the mind only. For example, consider an ethical law. Is it ever right to molest a child? No, you will say. But why? One can cite various reasons why, but at the end of the day, you are left espousing a principle which says simply that it is wrong. End of story.

Now an ethical law is not something that you can put under a microscope. You cannot take a photograph of a principle. Yet, they are real in every sense of that term. They are things that you perceive with the heart and mind and soul alone. They are—in Plato's words—the forms.

The significance of this claim cannot be overstated. It is the defining difference between a materialist philosophy and a non-materialist philosophy. This difference has defining ramifications across the entire spectrum of human activity—science, psychology, politics, economics, morality etc. It sets apart the person who believes in this claim from the one who does not believe in it. Of course, no one person might be 100% in one camp or the other. Often, it is a question of degree. Somebody, for example, may be 60% of one and 40% of the other, or vice versa.

What are the wellsprings that produce the claim that the world which we see and hear and feel and touch is not the only world and not the most important world? Where does this claim come from in the human spirit? Is it just an escapism from this perishable, changeable world? Or does it originate in a nobility of the human spirit that seeks to be unlocked? Is the world a better place with these beliefs, or are the materialist beliefs better—more pragmatic, more down to earth, more in conformity with the way things are? We shall be exploring these and more questions as we wend our way through the depths of history and the human spirit.

It should be noted that although Plato and others held these beliefs, it does not mean that they implemented them completely in practice. Plato, for example, had slaves. But nevertheless, his was a great intellectual achievement—one that inspired others for close to 2,000 years—and even today. Succeeding thinkers would spell out the consequences of his claim.

We know that he had been influenced by the ideas of Hinduism, which had similar notions, though cast in a different cultural mould. One legend has it that Plato even went to India, but it is more likely that these Hindu ideas traveled along the dusty caravan trade routes.

But whereas Hindu ideas were significantly cast in religious terms, Plato's were decidedly secular. He argued on the basis of reason, and this in some way makes his claim more compelling.

And significantly, the highest form of all was the form of the good. Because it was the highest, it could never be fully and completely explained by the lower forms. In significant part, however, it could be intuited by the human heart working in tandem with our faculty of reason.

The second central theme of this culture was that there were universal laws of ethics. Clearly, this is related to the first claim about the nature of reality. For Plato and succeeding generations, ethics were not subjective, relative or changeable. There was an absolute justice. This may not be always easy to find, but nevertheless the concept of justice was not infinitely malleable. There was a right and there was a wrong. Intellectual clarity demanded no less.

It was not always easy for Plato and his followers to discern actually what was right in a given situation. This, of course, is where Socrates' dialectic came in. By relentlessly questioning, the belief was that the truth would be eventually mined.

The third theme also follows from the previous two, and surfaces later on in Plato's thought—the existence of God. While Plato enunciated it in abstract terms, later generations such as the Christians, would seize on it to the fullest. Augustine, the 4th century bishop of Hippo in North Africa, would seek to baptize Plato's thought, in order to show that it was fully congruent with Christian teaching.

These three shaping ideas would define the heights of Western culture for the next 2000 years. While these ideas, at times, may have been honored more in their breach than their practice, nevertheless they created an overarching system of beliefs that nobody seriously questioned until the beginning of the new era. Rulers continued to slaughter millions, the predator class continued to strip the many of their land and possessions—all the while paying lip service to these three fundamental truths. This shows that one of the fundamental challenges facing much of humanity is to align action with professed belief. Until that day comes, havoc will reign on the earth.

One of the most egregious examples of this is an institution that came to dominate much of the Western world in the Middle Ages—the Catholic Church. Beginning with Jesus of Nazareth—who had nowhere to lay his head—it grew over succeeding centuries into the richest and most powerful institution in the West. Its monasteries and lands would be the envy of any earthly ruler. Yet it preached the doctrine that this life was merely a preparation for the next, that in this vale of tears we should place no importance on material possessions.

Yet, this institution degenerated to the point where little children ran around the sumptuous halls of the Vatican shouting "Papa", and by that they did not simply intend a honorific title. At least one pope had a mistress.

It was this corruption that led to the first crack in the Platonic synthesis. Martin Luther, horrified at the corruption which he saw in the Catholic Church, concluded that it could not be reformed from within, and that only a new church could solve that problem.

But, in the process, he uttered a claim that would reverberate around the world. It was that the individual would determine the truth in his or her mind. This implied that there was no "truth"—contrary to the claim of Plato. If one said that reality is more than matter, and another said that reality is only matter, truth is what you feel in your heart and mind. Truth is subjective. As he said at the Diet of Worms in 1521, "Here I stand, I can do no other".

He failed to realize, however, that his claim that truth was subjective was in conflict with some of his fundamental beliefs and actions. He claimed that corruption was wrong, that all should believe this, and that anybody who held the contrary was wrong. Yet, if truth is subjective, the claim that corruption is inherently wrong is incompatible with a claim that truth is subjective. Yet a revolution is born on this contradiction, and it would touch millions.

Simultaneously, a second force was at work. Western science had been born in the 6th. century B.C. in Miletus, a Greek colony in what is modern day Turkey. Thales is credited with asking the first modern, scientific question. Instead of asking which god or goddess did this or that, he asked "what?"—what is everything made of? His solution was nothing less than brilliant for his day—everything is made of water. It flows like a liquid, it becomes solid when it is frozen, and it becomes air when it is heated.

Implicit in this approach was the principle of empirical verification. His theory could be tested empirically. One did not have to take his claim on blind faith. If his theory did not test out empirically, it could be replaced by another. Whereas, if one said that Zeus was angry, how could one verify this?

Modern science was born.

Democritus, for example,—who has nothing to do with democracy—noticed that a flight of steps in Athens was gradually being worn away as people walked up and down them. Yet, he noted, we do not see any particles being worn away. Hence, he brilliantly concluded, the steps and everything else is made of invisible particles, and the Greek word for invisible particle was "atom". He is the father of modern atomic theory.

But this scientific approach developed slowly over the coming centuries. It was, as it were, in a period of gestation. It was only to burst into full bloom about 2000 years later. The single most important manifestation of that was Copernicus's claim that the earth went around the sun, not the sun around the earth.

This was truly earth shattering. The medieval view had been that the earth was the center of the universe, and that man was the center of earth. In one fell swoop, Copernicus had shattered this belief, and succeeding developments in astronomy would expand on that and show that earth is but a tiny piece of rock on the outer reaches of the universe. Man was reduced to seeming insignificance—a tiny, two-legged piece of life that lived for a few seconds in the immensity of time and the universe. There was no grandeur to this existence. Man for all intents and purposes was meaningless—flotsam in a universe of supernova, irrelevant to the life of billions of stars and galaxies.

A third and related force was being born into this tumultuous period, which would have an equally profound impact on the consciousness of man—capitalism.

There is obviously no exact date for the birth of capitalism. Contrary to some popular opinion, capitalism has not always been the economic system of humanity. In the guild system of the Middle Ages, the guild set the price of, for example, shoes. It would allow for the cost of materials and the labor of the cobbler, and set the price accordingly. Under capitalism, the price would be set to maximize profit—not just make a profit, but maximize it.

If any date can be assigned to the birth of capitalism, a good choice would be when Anton Fugger, a German weaver, began to purchase the products of other weavers, and then sell the cloth himself. It is estimated that he had about 1000 weavers producing for him at his peak.

When you control the products in any market, you increase your ability to set the price at the level you want—to maximize your profit.

Capitalism was a product of the emerging materialist psyche. Business had always sought to make a profit. Mercantilism in both Christian and Moslem countries strove to do that.

But with capitalism, there began the out and out quest for the maximization of profit. The focus once again was on the individual as an individual, as it was with Martin Luther and science. With the latter, it was the perceptions of the individual scientist that were central.

In time, this led to the questioning of the three fundamental tenets of Plato's synthesis. This did not happen overnight. Descartes was the first to raise these fundamental questions. He confronted them, but eventually found a way to accept them. But his solution opened the door for thinkers after him to question, and then reject, Plato's claims.

When Descartes sat down in his study and vowed not to get up until he had found the answer to his doubts, he laid the groundwork for others to arrive at a different conclusion. He asked what he could know with absolute certainty, and quickly concluded that all sense impressions could not meet that standard. There could be, for example, an evil demon controlling his mind. See the movie, "The Matrix"

At the end of the day, he concluded that the one thing which he could not doubt was his own existence—I doubt therefore I exist—or more popularly, I think therefore I exist. Crucially, however, he had already concluded that as he could not be sure that he had a body, he must be a thinking thing—a non-material entity. He had thus preserved the first tenet of Plato that what is most real is what is non-physical, non-material.

From there, it was only a few short steps before he claimed to conclude with absolute certainty that there was a God. While he did not focus significantly on ethics, his holding of two of Plato's assertions would have led him to assert that there are universal ethical standards.

But Descartes' questioning had opened the door, and others would reach a different conclusion.

The first major figure to do so was John Locke. His major attack on Plato's synthesis was that all ideas came from experience—that ideas are faint copies of sense impressions. This was a major attack on Plato's claim that what is truly real—the forms—are those non-physical, non-material entities such as the idea of justice. In short, Locke was creating a materialist philosophy.

However, he did not go the entire course. He still claimed that there must be a God. It was up to others after him to go down that road. Berkeley—a bishop—sought to solve the riddle by claiming that material things did not exist, that everything was simply an idea. He said that our experience would not change, just our explanation of it.

It was David Hume who drove the stake into the heart of Plato's thought. He agreed with Locke—albeit with some modifications—that all ideas come from experience. He was an agnostic—not an atheist—with regard to the question of God's existence. He decreed that reason is but the slave of the passions, and hence concluded that ethics is based on feelings—and thus cannot be universal as feelings vary with the individual and over time.

Thus in one fell swoop, Hume demolished Plato's synthesis and replaced it with a materialistic philosophy—the implications of which are still being worked out today. There was, however, one major attempt to refute him, and that was by Immanuel Kant, who stated that reading Hume's philosophy woke him from his dogmatic slumbers.

In brief—because Kant's work is very profound and deep—Kant can be seen as the modern Plato with 2000 years of history having flowed underneath the bridge. In his own unique and brilliant way, he argued for all three of Plato's claims.

His moral philosophy has had the greatest impact, and is of greatest concern to the modern materialist mind because it claims that each individual is possessed of infinite dignity and worth, and can never be treated as a means only, but must always be treated as an end in itself.

This is troublesome to the modern materialist philosophy because the latter in its revolt against the Platonic synthesis sought to secure acceptance—at least in part—by positioning itself on the side of the individual, and as a liberating force from the prior philosophy. Kant's philosophy presented a major challenge because it raised the fundamental question of how can a person be of inestimable worth if he or she is only a bunch of matter. What is so noble about a bunch of electrons, protons and neutrons? As we shall see, this will haunt the modern mind.

The 19th. and 20th. centuries were largely a working out of the implications of a materialist philosophy—except for one or two lone voices such as Kierkegaard. He argued that we should believe in a God precisely because it was irrational. But the majority—Nietzsche, Sartre, Camus—concluded that life is meaningless, and wrestled with what to do in face of that reality. The universe is irrational, we are irrational, and that is the way it is.

This would be reflected in art, music, psychology—the entire gamut of human experience. It would lead individuals to grab life with all the gusto they could—which often meant pursuing wealth and pleasure in an attempt to fill the metaphysical hole at the heart of their existence.

It is reflected in the madness of two world wars where millions slaughtered millions. It is reflected in the current phenomenon of nuclear weapons, where we have the ability to destroy planet earth 100 times over. So, if we do not get it right the first time, we still have 99 more chances.

It is reflected in the reality that an estimated 15,000 children die every day who do not have to die, because of malnutrition and the concomitant diseases that ravage the human body, while other children play games on I-Pads, PSPs, and all sorts of fancy electronic equipment. If we were starving, would we want others to spend their money on movies, basketball games etc. instead of trying to provide food for us?

So, in this mad, mad world, is there any hope, any solution? The succeeding chapters will explore this question.

CHAPTER 2

THE ECONOMY

It is axiomatic that all human beings—no matter what their abilities or lack thereof—are entitled to an appropriate share of the planet's resources in order to have adequate food, housing, clothing, education and health care., and to contribute to that endeavor according to their ability. Is that the case currently?

No.

The figures are overwhelming. On a global scale, 0.5% of the world's population control over 35% of the world's wealth. 2% of the world's population own 50% of the world's wealth. India has 55 billionaires worth $250 billion. That is about one sixth of the annual economic output of the entire country. And yet strikingly, only about 3% of the population of India have incomes higher than the very poorest of Americans. (The Haves and The Have-Nots, p. 118, Branko Milanovic) Putting it another way, the top 10% of income recipients receive 56% of the world's income, while the poorest 10% receive a mere 0.7% of global income. The former have 80 times more income than the latter. (Milanovic p. 152) To put this in perspective, it would take the poor two hundred years to make what the rich make in a year.

The richest 1% in the world number about 60 million. 29 million of these are Americans, 4 million Germans, 3 million British, French and Italian each, 2 million Canadians, Koreans, Japanese and Brazilians, 1 million Swiss, Spaniards, Australian, Dutch, Taiwanese, Chileans and Singaporeans. There are no statistically significant numbers from Africa, China, India or East Europe. (Milanovic p. 169).

Absolute poverty was defined by the World Bank in 2005 as living on $1.25 per day in the U.S., buying U.S. goods. With that, you could buy a McDouble at McDonald's (99 cents plus 9 cents tax, leaving 16 cents for housing, clothing, health care, education and other food). Try it for a week in order to get some idea of what it is like. Currently. Almost 1 billion people live in absolute poverty. Another 2 billion live on less than $2 a day.

In Niger and Mali, 9 out of 10 people live on less than $2 per day. This has to cover food, clothing and shelter. There is nothing for medical care and education. In the dark alleys that lie behind the glitz of Hong Kong, tens of thousands live in "cage homes" or "coffin homes", which average about 15 square feet in size. Meanwhile, high end properties go for $10,550 per square foot.

In the U.S., 1% of the population owns approximately 50% of the wealth. Their fellow Americans have to share the remaining half. But the figures are even more disturbing regarding the super-rich—those who make at least $2 million a year. Though they comprise only 0.1%

of the population, they control 10% of the economy and their wealth is increasing dramatically. Despite all this, 90% of the $1.3 trillion in Bush's 2001 income tax cuts went to the top 5% of the country. Indeed, in the U.S., government is by the rich, for the rich and of the rich.

Why this disparity?

Jacob Hacker, a Yale political science professor, believes it is because this group pressured Congress to deregulate the financial services industry, allowing it to engage in extreme risk-taking and bigger profits. In effect, as 3 Citigroup analysts wrote in 2005, a plutonomy—an economy controlled by the rich—emerged. Despite the recession and despite being significantly responsible for causing that recession, the big guns on Wall Street took home more than ever in 2010. In 1988, the average income of a taxpayer was $33,400 according to the IRS. 20 years later in 2008, the average income fell to $33,000—and price of everything has risen. The income of the richest Americans has risen 33% during the same period. In 2006, Merrill Lynch paid $500 million in bonuses to just 100 employees.

Even though the economic picture in the U.S. is dire, much of the rest of the world would be only too glad to have it. On a global basis, the U.S. owns about 25% of the world's wealth—$50 trillion of an estimated $200 trillion. Yet it has only about 4.5% of the world population. Of the 1000 people on planet earth who own more than $5 billion, 3 out of 4 live in America. It is estimated that if everybody lived on the same standard of living as Americans, it would require 9 planet earths to do that.

World Bank economist Branko Milanovic in his book, The Haves and the Have-Nots, states that approximately half of the richest 1% in the world—about 29 million—live in the U.S. A person is in that top 1% if he or she earns $34,000 a year after taxes. The global median income is $1,225 a year. The figures are adjusted for different costs of living in the world.

These numbers could be replicated endlessly.

Leaving aside any considerations of morality, is this a desirable situation? Clearly not. As the capitalistic economic engine relies on growth, growth is ultimately stymied by the fact that the 3 billion plus who live on less than $2 a day cannot purchase a T.V., a toaster—or any similar product. When one tosses morality into the equation, the conclusion is a no-brainer. Capitalism both practically and ethically is wrong. Capitalism is not a capital idea.

Ethically, all human beings are entitled to an equal share of the planet's resources. No God or law granted a lion's share to the few. Everybody is entitled as a matter of right to that amount of the resources of the planet sufficient for proper food, clothing, housing, education and health care. Currently, that is clearly not the case on planet earth. Proper does not mean minimum, Every day, for instance, children die of malnutrition—their distended bellies a grotesque sign not of too much food, but of too little and of too poor a quality. Medically, when a child's upper arm measures less than 11cm in circumference, the chances of survival are slim or none.

Capitalism also pits one human against another. Inevitably, this creates strife, conflict and war. We are all in one lifeboat together. We must all work together. One person cannot throw another overboard in order to secure a better position for him or herself. Everybody has a right to be in that boat. The ultimate, inevitable consequence of adopting a policy of every person for himself, is that the boat will capsize and all will drown.

The very existence of enough nuclear weapons to destroy planet earth 100 times over is a grim reminder that this possibility is no more than 20 minutes away—the time for one nuclear missile to reach an adversary's homeland.

The fact is that we are meant to work together, not fight against each other. The argument that competition is good is short-term and short-sighted. Yes, it might make a better widget here and a better gadget there in the short run, but ultimately, the only true benefit is when the insights and ingenuities of all are able to be contributed to the human endeavor. How many inventions, how many cures, how many great pieces of music or art, are forever lost because those people were not allowed to contribute to the system because of its inequalities? At the end of the day, capitalism makes us poorer, not richer.

At this moment in history, this is particularly true for what has been regarded as the bastion of capitalism—the U.S.

For much of the 19th. and 20th. centuries, capitalism in the U.S. produced an abundance of goods. This success was made possible by a variety of factors, including conditions in other parts of the world. But one significant factor was the availability of cheap labor through immigration. In this light, the inscription on the Statue of Liberty takes on a somewhat different meaning— "give me your tired, your poor, your huddled masses". As Howard Zinn documents so clearly in his "Peoples' History of the United States", these people were paid rock-bottom wages.

As workers began to organize for better wages and working conditions, wages began to rise, and the key to the economic success of the U.S. was the consistent rise in wages paid to its workers. This raised the living standards of many Americans—not all, but many. As Henry Ford realized, if he paid his workers more, they could buy more of his cars.

But eventually the capitalistic system began to see its profits diminish. Always foraging for ways to maximize profits, and taking advantage of changed conditions in the global environment, these flag-waving capitalists began to move manufacturing "off-shore"—as it was euphemistically called—beginning in the early 70's. If a self-respecting capitalist could get somebody to make a product for $2 a day, instead of for $20 an hour, the answer was crystal clear—go "off-shore". The labor cost to make an I-Phone in China is $7.80. In the U.S. it is $168. Ominously, in 1971 for the first time, the U.S. had a trade deficit—it was importing more than it was exporting. By 1986, the trade deficit had grown to $140 billion. For the first time since the Great Depression, the 1970's saw no increase in American manufacturing jobs.

As Jeffrey Madrick points out in his "The End of Affluence", prior to 1973, the average rate of growth in the U.S. economy was 3.4% a year. Since 1973, the average has been just a little more than 2% a year. (p. 4-6). He projects that by the year 2013, that translates into a loss of $35 trillion for the U.S. economy—a loss of more than $100,000 for each and every American. No wonder that there are cries of pain across the land. And why such a loss? Primarily because America's CEOs sent U.S. jobs "offshore"—a nice euphemism for the thousands of miles of intervening ocean.

And so the exodus of jobs began. In response to critics who worried that the U.S. was draining itself of its economic potential, capitalists happily responded that the U.S. could become a service economy.

20 years later in the 1990's, those service jobs began to migrate offshore also. Airlines established reservation centers in such places as Argentine and Brazil. Computer companies set up giant call centers in India. X-rays taken in the U.S. could be read more cheaply by a doctor thousands of miles away in India. (A number of years ago, the University of California outsourced its employee medical records to India. A lady there, who apparently had not been paid for several months, threatened to release all those medical files onto the internet if she was not paid at once. As those files were never released, she was seemingly paid. An interesting by-product of globalization.!)

Then, a seemingly paradoxical phenomenon happened. The low wage countries—especially China—began to export its products to the rich countries of the world. U.S. companies such as Wal-Mart (maybe more aptly named the Great Walmart of China!) became the conduit for these goods to the U.S. consumer.

The result? For example, July 4 might be more appropriately called Dependence Day. Almost all the fireworks and American flags are made in China. Of course, the money used to pay for these products goes back to China.

This caused no major problems as long as the U.S. consumer was paying for the products out of his/her own savings from the boom years. But as these savings dried up and were not being replenished because jobs were going overseas, the U.S. consumer eventually was borrowing money from China to pay for Chinese goods.

This interesting phenomenon began to happen in the early years of the 21st. century. As Chinese imports were paid for in the only reserve currency in the world—the U.S. dollar—China and other producing countries sought a safe location to invest their profits—and they thought there was no safer place than the U.S.

Money cascaded into the U.S. and banks scrambled to lend it left, right and center. One key area for lending was homes. The latter had always been seen as part of the American dream, and now banks—flush with all this money—encouraged Americans to borrow, borrow, borrow. Countless stories abound of a borrower asking for $300,000, and the bank asking "Why don't you take $350,000?" In many cases, all the borrower had to do was to state his or her income—not prove it—and subsequent investigations show that many borrowers simply vastly inflated their incomes to qualify for a higher loan. Add to this that many mortgages required the borrower to pay only the interest for the first 2 or 5 years, and the stage was set for disaster. The borrower thus had extra money in his pocket to buy the big screen T.V., take that vacation to Hawaii, buy a fancier car. You had a volatile mix that would erupt in the worst financial crisis since the Great Depression of the 1930's.

As demand was brisk, and as the loan brokers made handsome commissions on each mortgage, the price of homes kept rising astronomically—more than $10,000 a month in many cases. The party had begun, and consumers used their homes as ATM machines to buy all those consumer goodies that televisions and glossy magazines tantalizingly set before them. $7 trillion in mortgages was written between 2000 and 2007.

But when those short-term, interest—only mortgages came to an end, the party began to come an end also. Overnight, homeowners were faced with sharply higher mortgage payments because they now were required to begin paying down the principal—which they could not pay. They began to default on their mortgages, and homes cascaded onto the market, where there were no buyers. The rout had begun. House prices plummeted and the recession was in full swing. Investors were left holding hundreds of billions of dollars of bad debt.

It was further fueled by the credit default swaps in the financial markets. Essentially. firms like AIG and Lehman Brothers would say to investors— "Invest in this risky product because we will guarantee to repay you your money if it fails." And when investors in droves came pounding on their doors for payment, such companies were unable to pay. Lehman Brothers in its final week started out the week with $16 billion in the bank. By Friday, it had nothing.

These problems—and more—might be surmountable in an economy that is on the up-swing. But the harsh reality is that capitalism is gradually turning the U.S. into a third world country. It is not happening overnight, but the telltale signs are already appearing—decaying infrastructure such as roads and airports, calls for workers to take lower salaries and drastic cuts in things like health care benefits.

Though CEOs of capitalistic corporations might clasp their hand to their heart on July 4 as the Star Spangled Banner is played, they are in fact some of the most un-American of citizens because they are systematically draining the U.S. of its wealth and jobs, and transferring factories and facilities overseas.

The U.S. is on its way to becoming a third world country. Of course, it will take time, but the process is underway. Its infrastructure is crumbling. The I-10 freeway east of Los Angeles is a bone-jarring ride for commuters.

Airports such as Kennedy in New York look decrepit next to the gleaming airports of places like Malaysia, Singapore, Hong Kong, Beijing. Every month, the U.S. federal government has to borrow $124 billion just to pay its bills. Programs such as Medicare and Social Security are being slashed because "we cannot afford them any more." Everywhere, it is not expansion, but retrenchment

Its current federal debt is $14.3 trillion. $9.8 trillion of that is owned by Americans, $4.5 trillion by foreigners. Of the latter, China owns the largest share, $1.16 trillion—8% of the total.

Will the U.S. ever pay all that back? Without jobs, it cannot do so, and it will never have the jobs that it once had. Politicians rant about creating jobs, but nobody is going to pay anybody in the U.S. to do a job when the job can be done for a fraction of the cost in another country. And all this is a product of the economic system that the U.S. embraced wholeheartedly in its heyday. That system, capitalism, gives a country a brief day in the sunshine, but then mercilessly consigns it to the grip of winter.

Eventually, of course, the same process will happen to countries like China and India. As wages rise—which they are beginning to do so in China—companies will move to the next area of low cost wages—Vietnam, Thailand, Malaysia. In the last few years, 1000 shoe manufacturers have moved from China to Vietnam because the wages in the latter are lower.

These countries all have unemployment rates below 3%. One of the reasons for this according to experts is that a lot of investments that used to go to China, are now going to these countries because of low labor costs. Africa is probably the next area to get the investments and jobs.

There, the same process will be repeated. Already, there are two factories in Botswana which are making clothes for the U.S. market.

And one day, the jobs will come back to the U.S. again when its people are willing to work for 50 cents an hour.

This constant churning is a hallmark of capitalism—the perpetual quest, not for salvation, but for greater and greater profits. The capitalist is never at peace, never happy, because he or she always wants more.

The most influential U.S. critic of stock speculation is Warren Buffet. In the book, The Tao of Warren Buffet (2006, co-authored by Mary Buffet and David Clark), his scathing criticism of investment firms for focusing on short-term profit is boundless.

> "The trading madness that goes with the mutual and hedge funds is almost boundless . . . if there is even the slightest drop in earnings, they will sell the stock, and if there is even a modest rise in earnings, they buy it . . . This is not investing; it is speculating under the guise of investing. Investing is buying a piece of a business and watching it grow; speculating is throwing the dice on the short-term direction of the stock's price."

Beginning in the 1980's, these denizens of Wall Street gradually peeled away all the regulations that had been enacted in the Great Depression to restrict dangerous speculation that produced nothing.

The speculators—banks, hedge funds, private equity firms—invested trillions in incredibly high-risk ventures. It was as if Wall Street became a Las Vegas casino.

The capitalist preaches freedom. But what does this mean? In reality, it means the pursuit of self-interest. By definition, if self-interest is one's leading motivation, conflict must inevitably ensue because one's self interest must necessarily clash with somebody else's. Yet the capitalist turns a blind eye to this simple truth. If the ordinary person were to seek to ban capitalism because it was not in his or her self-interest, what would the capitalist think then? Can one honestly argue that my pursuing my self-interest is in your self-interest? One needs to be a very good salesperson to sell that one. George Soros made a billion almost overnight by betting that the value of the English pound would drop, and basically forced it to drop, causing great damage to millions of English citizens. He did the same in the Asian crisis and caused a deep recession and forced countries to cut their social spending to secure IMF funding to bail them out.

The irony is that the overwhelming majority of people under capitalism are not free. In reality, what a capitalist wants is monopoly, and in a monopoly you are not free. If there is only one airline, that airline can charge whatever it wants. The whole purpose of a monopoly is to remove freedom of choice for people. The ultimate capitalist is the one who owns everything—grocery stores, banks, dry-cleaners, dentists, doctors—you name it. As Henry Simons wrote in 1948:

> "The great enemy of democracy is monopoly . . . A monopolist is an implicit thief . . . because his possession of market power leads to the exchange of commodities at prices that do not reflect underlying social scarcities." (Quoted in Age of Greed, p. 35.)

We see here again one of the ultimate ironies of history. A beautifully sounding word—in this case, freedom—is used to promote its exact opposite. But nobody is truly free unless all are free. One is not exercising ones freedom when one is diminishing the freedom of another. The true conservative is the one who conserves the freedom of everybody else. The true liberal is the one who liberates everybody else.

As long as one knows that billions suffer in poverty and degradation, one's heart and mind can never be free. We can try to submerge that reality deep into our unconscious, but we are made such that that our unconscious will bedevil us in a thousand ways. Ultimately, there is no escaping the truth, and it is only the truth that sets us free.

This gets us to center of capitalism—the stock market.

The stock market is where those with money in excess of what they need to live, seek to use that excess to make more money by lending it to others—companies and governments. And they seek the greatest possible profit consistent with their willingness to take a risk. In general, the greater the risk, the greater the possibility of higher profit—and of course, failure.

To read the inside story of Wall Street is to become sick at the stomach. It is a story of unabashed, naked greed by all the players. Wall Street would more aptly be called Greed Street. A lot of its major players are from our allegedly greatest universities—Harvard, Yale, Columbia etc. and this is a damning indictment of the education that they provide.

And what happens in the financial market is all determined by the quest for greater and greater profits. Goldman Sachs, Morgan Stanley are but a few of the players whose unbridled greed has caused the downfall of the U.S. Wall Street has done more harm to the U.S. than all the attacks of 9/11. Al Quaeda could not have wished for a better friend.

There is a fundamental inconsistency at the heart of our current financial system. Investors want to amass as large an amount of money as possible. That money has to come from other people. But the less that those people are left with, the less are they able to buy the products and services offered by the investors. The collision of these irreconcilable forces has to eventually cause a crisis, and this is going to be manifested in a recession (or in the worst case scenario—a depression.) Economists blithely talk about a recession as being an inevitable part of the business cycle without ever explaining how this happens.

It is greed once again on the part of the investors that leads to this recurring crisis. One way to handle this is to ensure that everybody is paid a living wage. This is to the advantage of all concerned. Workers get a decent wage, and can thus buy the products that the investor invests in. If workers only get starvation wages, then they cannot buy any products but the bare minimum. This only goes to show again that greed is not to the common good. Attempting to garner more than ones fair share is ultimately counterproductive.

Furthermore, as noted above, greed can be deadly, often in the literal sense of that term. For example, General Electric had dumped PCBs (polychlorinated biphenyls) into the Hudson River and other places in the 1960s and 70s. PCBs are a poisonous by-product of chemical processes. As of late 2010, GE has not paid for the clean up under the 1980 Superfund law, administered by the Environmental Protection Agency. GE keeps the money. Others are damaged because of that.

Greed makes peace impossible, and guarantees strife. It may well be humanity's biggest single challenge. A materialistic philosophy guarantees greed, because it cannot provide any rationale for not being greedy. Only a non-materialistic philosophy can do that, because it provides for realities that are more important than material possessions. For example, the dignity of each human being is something that is beyond material calculation. As Kant said, dignity is beyond price.

In the world of investing, no non-material values are present. The golden rule of investing is to buy low and sell high. But consider this. If you buy low, you must think that the value of the stock is greater than what the seller thinks. If you sell high, you must think that the value of the stock is less than what you are selling it for. In both cases, you are seeking to rip-off the other party.

Is this any way to run planet earth—to have it run by one person ripping off another? Is this a recipe for harmony and peace, or a recipe for strife and war?

This is why every so many years, capitalism has recessions. There can only be so much ripping off before the system tanks—it topples in on itself. Then it will go through a painful period where some of these inequities are worked out, and then it will start all over again. In the process, however, many lose their jobs, and there is much suffering among the people of the world.

The irony of ironies in these situations is that on the one hand, these grasping, greedy capitalists seek to do away with any financial regulations that curb their insatiable appetites, and yet on the other hand, when that financial disaster strikes which they produced, those same grasping greedy hands, without blinking an eye, take the public's money to bail themselves out. They privatize all the gains for themselves but seek to socialize the losses on the taxpayer. For example, General Electric which had plunged into the subprime mortgage lending business in the early 2000's, incurred massive losses in the 2008 meltdown. Its stock dropped 60%. Yet the public through the Federal Deposit Insurance Corporation agreed to guarantee close to $140 billion of its debts because General Electric owned a small federal bank.

This intensifying greed has led Wall Street over the last 40 years to focus more and more on short term profits. By whatever means—fair or foul—drive up the price of a stock. Why? Because the remuneration for the big guns was significantly based on stock options. Hence, if you could drive up the price of your company's stock, you could cash in on your stock options big time. Boesky, Milken, Soros, Weill—all became billionaires this way. Stock options should not be allowed as compensation for anybody. They create an inherent conflict of interest.

But this artificial inflating of a stock is no way to run an economy. It results in one boom and bust after another. Those responsible for the boom and bus profit in either case. It is the ordinary citizen who suffers when workers are laid off. The quest for short terms profits resulted in bad loans, poor financing decisions, and terrible advice for investors. As Jeff Madrick states in his book "Age of Greed",

> "The 1990s through 2002 was the most corrupt "decade" since the 1920s—and one of the most corrupt in American business history. An infrastructure of corruption, whose seeds blossomed with Mike Milken, Ivan Boesky, and the savings and loan entrepreneurs in the 1980s, spread in the 1990s across

the American establishment into elite professions, including commercial and investment banks, accountants, lawyers, consultants, ratings agencies, and mutual funds as well as newer hedge funds." (Page 320)

For example, as Mr. Madrick documents, research analysts were supposed to be objective and independent. Yet, in 1990, a senior financial officer at Morgan Stanley wrote that,

"—the pay of research analysts at Morgan be directly linked to how much underwriting, brokerage, or asset management business the company they were covering did with Morgan Stanley" (p. 321)

Earnings were repeatedly manipulated to boost stock prices. Jack Welch at GE Capital used pension fund reserves to increase quarterly earnings. That is why its stock rose five-fold between 1995 and 2000. Companies reported one set of figures in their financial statements, and another to the IRS. Enron said it had earnings of $1.8 billion in 1999 in its financial statements, but told the IRS that it had lost $1 billion.

Time and again in the 1990's, CEOs perpetrated major frauds but hardly anybody went to jail. Dean Buntrock, CEO of Waste Management, cooked the books by $1.7 billion, was sued by the SEC, but settled for a $20 million fine without having to admit that he did anything wrong. That was a pittance, given the immense wealth which he had. If an ordinary citizen stole a pack of chewing gum from a 7-Eleven store, he would end up in jail. Being rich has its privileges. It is estimated investors lost at least $4 trillion in the period 1990-2002.

Ironically, the media uses the terms "privileged" and "less fortunate" to describe peoples' economic standing in the world. This is a gross misuse of language—no doubt engineered by those who want their true status to be concealed. Wall Street crooks are not "privileged". They secured their wealth by stealing. When will we call a spade a spade?

Likewise, somebody is "less fortunate"—not because some sort of fortune or divine fate put them there, though that is what the language intimates—but in many cases, because the greedy took from them. It is sometimes said that he or she who controls the language, controls the world.

Beginning in the 1980's, the compensation of CEOs was increasingly composed of generous stock options. This created a powerful conflict of interest. A CEO's financial interest clearly lay in securing the raising of the stock price of the company. As investors looked primarily to the quarterly earnings report to gauge the value of the company's stock, a CEO had a strong incentive to manipulate the books to maximize the earnings report. After the Enron scandal in 2000, 400 hundred companies had to "restate" their earnings that year. That means that they had to tell the truth. If CEOs were banned from receiving stock options, there would be a lot more honesty in the marketplace. In 1970, the average CEO compensation was 25 times higher than the average production worker. By 1990, it was 100 times. By 1996, 210 times.

Consider the word "investor". How do "investors" get their extra money?

The answer in its simple form is from the pockets of others. It is certainly legitimate for the maker of a product to include the cost of production of that item (raw materials, labor, overhead etc.) in the selling price. It is also legitimate to include enough to provide the manufacturer with what he or she needs to live a decent life with adequate food, shelter, clothing, health care and education.

But when the sales price of the product goes beyond that, it moves into the area of gouging. Every dollar that is gouged from another increases the economic instability of the world. The world was not made to have "Haves and Have-Nots", but that everybody be a "Have."

Sam Walton, founder of Wal-Mart, became the richest man in the U.S.—worth an estimated $20 billion in those days. He did so in significant part by paying his workers minimum wage. Many Wal-mart workers had to get their health care through Medicaid—in effect, charging the general public for it. A number of years ago, a study concluded that in California alone, the use of Medicaid by Wal-mart workers cost the taxpayers $70 million a year.

It is hard to understand how somebody who had so much wealth could pay his workers so little, and look at himself in the mirror in the morning. What was wrong with his heart? His humanity? Are there minimum Americans and maximum Americans? Is this the ideal of how an American should treat a fellow American—or any human being? Didn't he know what standard of living his minimum wages would inflict on his workers in terms of housing, education, food, health care etc.? A very sad commentary on America.

So, a more appropriate word for "investors" might be "gougers". That is not very nice, but what they do is not very nice. Yes, that system has produced IPods and IPads etc., but it has also produced more than 3 billion people who live on less than $2 a day.

These are not pleasant facts. In general, we tend to recoil from using harsh language to describe others. But the reality is even more unpleasant. To those living in squalid conditions and with little or no food, the reality is more than unpleasant—it is deadly. Yet, Josette Sheeran, executive director of the United Nations' World Food Programme, said a 17-cent package of nutrients with a chickpea base can meet the needs of a hungry infant, and more than enough food is grown to feed everyone. But still many wake up every day not knowing how they will be able to feed themselves.

Clearly, the current system has to change. The zillion dollar question then is whether there is an alternative.

Before that question can be answered, a series of other questions must be addressed such as what is an economy for, on what principles should it be organized, what is its role in human affairs.

In simple terms, an economy deals with the transformation of raw materials into objects to serve human purposes.

The following principles seem to be basic for any rational, humane economy.

First, those objects must first provide for adequate food, clothing, housing, education and health care for all people irrespective of income. Anything above these basics is classified as a luxury. As long as some people do not have basics, nobody should have luxuries.

Second, this transformation of the raw materials of the planet into usable items for humanity must not destroy the very planet from which they come. The current use of fossil fuels that is producing global warming is but one example. One study claims that if everybody lived on the same economic level as the U.S., we would need 9 planet earths to support that.

Third, all according to their ability, should contribute to providing these basics.

Fourth, there should be equal pay for equal work globally. Article 23 (2) of the Universal Declaration of Human Rights states "Everyone, without any discrimination, has the right to equal pay for equal work." A person who makes a pair of shoes in Jakarta, should be paid the same as somebody in Los Angeles. This principle alone will eliminate the constant churning that capitalism engages in. Capitalism is constantly seeking areas of low cost labor. Some companies are already moving out of China to other countries because the labor is cheaper in the latter.

Many Americans who hear this principle for the first time may well flinch. Does this mean that their standard of living will go down?

The answer is that it is going down already and the current capitalistic system guarantees that it will go down, not just further, but to rock bottom. The question is how far will it fall? This principle of equal pay for equal work ensures that it will fall no further than the standard of everybody else. Without this principle, it would fall even lower. When implemented, there will be no more third world countries. Without it, the U.S. will become a third world country. No more SUVs, wide-screen T.Vs, I-Phones, I-Pods, and whatever other I-Things are out there. (It is not uninteresting that Apple has an "I" in front of so many of its products. It emphasizes the focus on the individual.)

Fifth, there should be an approximately equal level of wealth for all. Inequalities breed animosities and resentment. U.S. basketball star, Kobe Bryant, made more than $216,000 a game in 2006. It takes the average U.S. grade school teacher approximately 4 years to earn what Kobe Bryant earns in one night, and who serves the more important function in a society? His current income this year is about $34.5 million

Sixth, the individual creativity and enterprise of all should be promoted consistent with the requirements of a just society. No one group, government or private, has or should have a monopoly on creativity and enterprise.

Seventh, competition should be encouraged, but can never undermine cooperation.

The question then is how to structure such an economy.

The capitalist answer is profit. It claims that we are all selfish and therefore should appeal to it to produce economic growth. As discussed earlier, whether that will even work is problematical. Yes, capitalism can point to significant economic growth for some under its aegis. People have I-Pods and I-Phones because of it, yes, but even greater numbers do not have food, or shelter or education or health care. Which is more important? The answer is obvious.

But there is another problem with capitalism. It asserts as a matter of fact that we are all irredeemably selfish. This is an empirical claim, and as such, can be empirically tested. While it is obvious that we can be selfish, are we always selfish, and irredeemably so?

Examples of the opposite spring to mind—the soldier who gives his life for his country, the parent who sacrifices for their child. Are they deep down really being selfish? Is the soldier who throws himself on the hand grenade to save the lives of buddies, getting something out of it? Not plausibly, unless you regard being blown to smithereens as getting something out of it. If the capitalist then claims that the soldier MUST be getting something out of it, the capitalist has moved beyond an empirical claim (psychological egoism) to an ideology—which is a belief held despite evidence to the contrary. Once the capitalist does that, we lose all interest in his claim, because I could equally make the claim that deep down, we are all altruists, despite the evidence to the contrary.

The fact is that there have been societies where individual profit was not the engine of the economy. In traditional Hawaiian society, for example, everybody pulled together as a group, and nobody went hungry or homeless. They had no need of a Welfare Department. Whether that model would work in our modern society is a separate question. But it does undercut a central claim of capitalism that all people are ultimately selfish.

This philosophy grows out of the materialistic mindset that ushered in the modern world. If we are just flesh and bones, particles in motion, pleasure-seeking entities, then it is hard to argue that we can be unselfish. The new mindset is probably best summed up in the phrase advocated by the apostles of materialism "Greed is Good". In the Middle Ages, greed was one of the 7 deadly sins. Yet, such a dominant figure of the financial world as Alan Greenspan had written in 1965 that the greed of the businessman is "the unexcelled protector of the consumer." (Age of Greed, p. 228)

And greed is not just deadly for an individual. It is deadly for a society as well. Greed is what has brought down every society in the past which has engaged in it—whether it be the Sumerians, Romans, British, and now Americans. It will be the same in the future for every society that is greedy. Greed is ultimately self-destructive. If one takes more than should be taken, reality will seek to restore that balance in its own way.

Does greed come from the materialistic mindset, or does greed produce the materialistic mindset? As with all such questions, the better answer is probably both. Rather there is an interlocking relationship between them, one feeding off the other. Having said that, it is probably greed that has the greater influence. It is no coincidence that the emergence of the materialistic mindset occurs at the dawn of the colonization of the world by the European powers. Why did they colonize? Greed pure and simple. They wanted other peoples' land and resources—and in some cases, their people as slaves. Until humanity confronts its greed, the majority of the world will always be in need. Today, more than 3 billion people live in grinding poverty, and almost 1 billion of those in extreme poverty, where they cannot be sure if they will even get enough food for the day.

But if we are more than matter, if there is something in us that can transcend matter, then it would seem that we are not irredeemably selfish and greedy. We may be selfish many times, or even most of the time, but we are not made so that we cannot but be selfish.

History and everyday life provide us with many inspiring examples of unselfishness. The priest in the concentration camp who substituted himself for execution instead of the Jewish father, saying, "You have children, I do not." The soldiers who give their lives for their countries—ironically for capitalistic interests sometimes. The ordinary, everyday acts of kindness which are done, not because the giver gets anything out of it, but for the sake of somebody else. An economic system that has such inherent flaws in its fundamental structure is rightfully subject to considerable skepticism.

Communism, while appealing in its concern for equality, limits the creativity of individuals by its top-down heavy approach. Creativity, resourcefulness, ingenuity are not the prerogatives of any state. By stifling the wellsprings of the human spirit with bureaucratic tape, it destroys the dynamism that is so essential to all human activity.

The one model that seems to sit in the middle of both these extreme, is the Scandinavian model (Denmark, Finland, Iceland, Norway, Sweden). While there are individual differences between these countries, the central features are high tax rates to distribute wealth (Sweden taxes at 51% of GDP—the U.S. is 26.9%) and strong social welfare safety nets (e.g. Denmark's wage-based unemployment benefits are around 90%).

In general, there is a good standard of living for all, and a generous safety net when things go wrong. While there are some disparities in wealth, they are nothing compared to those prevalent in the U.S. It is said that in some countries such as Norway, millionaires are frowned upon. It is reported that traffic fines are commensurate with net worth—much to the chagrin of a millionaire who received a $40,000 traffic fine.

The Scandinavian model seems to be a happy compromise between the extremes of capitalism and communism. Of course, those countries are relatively small compared to a country like the U.S., but in principle, that does not seem to matter. The people there seem relatively content with their system—not like the U.S. which is racked with social tensions arising out of poverty and the insecurities that go with it. There can be no real freedom where there is inequality, and the U.S. has a lot of inequality. Freedom and equality are inextricably linked. Where there is no equality, there is no freedom. Freedom is diminished in proportion as equality is diminished.

Of course, all these transitions will not happen overnight. However, we do not have the luxury of time. Over 3 billion people who live in grinding poverty cannot be expected to be patient forever. Not one should die unnecessarily. Their situation is so dire that it needs remedying NOW. If we were in their shoes, we should think the same.

Humanity has great problems facing it, many of which have been allowed to fester from time immemorial. Each day that they are allowed to gather momentum, is a day when it becomes harder to solve them. We have hope commensurate with the challenges, but there can come a point when those challenges can crush hope, and then we all lose.

From a commonsense standpoint, the economy of the world can be handled efficiently if it is based on solid, ethical principles. There is no need for one nation to strive against another. We are all in the same lifeboat, and each person is infinitely precious.

To ensure this, we need a cap on income. As stated above, basketball star, Kobe Bryant, made $216,082 per game in 2006—and this does not include bonuses, incentives or pay for playoff games. He is undoubtedly a great player, but should society allow anybody to make this much when more than 3 billion people live in grinding poverty of less than $2 a day?

Of course, he is only able to make so much because he takes more out of other peoples' pockets. The average regular game ticket price for the Lakers in 2011 was $175. And that is just the average price. Clearly, that money could have been spent on something else. Admittedly, the fans "chose" to pay that money, but the fact that they did, shows the power of advertising and brainwashing.

Whatever the ceiling should be on salaries is obviously a good question. But that there should be a ceiling is clearly unquestionable—at least as long as there is so much poverty in the world. People are dying every day from malnutrition and its effects.

But one may argue—people like Kobe Bryant train hard to be a good player. Yes, but we have to remember that he was not the cause of the body that he was given at birth which enables him to be such a great player. He developed it, of course, but the "basic equipment" was already in place. The fact that somebody was born with a great brain or great body or great beauty does not mean that they can harvest for themselves an unfair amount of the world's resources. We are predominantly who we are because of what we have been given, not because of what we did.

Yes, some may say, but these people often give a lot to charity. That is good, but the world should be structured so that there is no need for charity. Furthermore, are some people able to give to charity because they siphoned more than they should from others?

Bill Gates, currently the second richest man in the world ($56 billion), has given $28 billion to charity, and administers a charitable foundation of $37.1 billion. This sounds as if he would be an instant candidate for canonization as a saint if he were a Catholic. But some of you from your

U.S. history may have learned of a product called Windows 98. When it came out in 1998, many analysts valued it at about $40. Yet it sold for $89.95. That extra $49.95 is termed monopoly profits—something that you can demand from purchasers because you control the market. At that time, approximately 95% of the world's computers ran on Windows. Is this "charity" akin to somebody coming into your house, stealing $100, then giving you $10 on the way out? A harsh comparison, but is it true?

In other words, how much of that $56 billion fortune was ethically earned? Even if you control the market place, should you charge more than a fair price—that is the cost of production plus a reasonable profit—however the latter is determined?

A cap on income would give society a say on how much any individual should be allowed to keep. A truly human being would be only too glad to welcome such a ceiling when they see the tremendous poverty and suffering in the world. We have a long way to go down the road before we become truly human.

Our humanity is diminished as long as there are enough resources—which there are—on planet earth to feed, clothe, shelter, educate and take care of everybody, and as long as even one person dies because he or she cannot get access to those resources. Imagine how much our humanity is diminished when more than 3 billion fellow human beings live in grinding poverty. As Gandhi said, "Poverty is the worst form of violence".

Obviously, to make the wrenching change from our current avaricious system to one of fairness and justice is not easy. But it has to be done—and we cannot kick the can down the road by saying that we will come up with a 20 year plan or a 40 year plan. We need action now. If we were starving now, what would we think if somebody told us that they had a 20 year plan to solve the problem? We would say, naturally, "but I need food now. I will be dead in 20 years." Shockingly, the administration of George W. Bush proclaimed that food is a goal or aspiration to be realized progressively and it translates into the opportunity to secure food: it is not a guaranteed entitlement. It simultaneously held that civil and political rights are 'inalienable and immediately enforceable'. Ir did not explain how one can have civil and political rights if one does not have food. Presumably, breathing is not a guaranteed right also, just an aspiration. Wait around 20 years, and you will have the resources to breathe. http://www.humanrights-usa.net/statements/0421Food.htm. Reasonable people may disagree on how best to make this transition. But on one thing, no reasonable person can disagree. Everybody has to have adequate food, shelter, clothing, education and health care. That is a basic minimum for all.

In this regard, one institution that says noble things about poverty and social justice—the Catholic church—is in an incongruous position. Probably nowhere in the world is there a greater collection of gold, jewels and other precious objects than in the Vatican. Now, if the Vatican earned more from those vast possessions than the possessions are worth, there might be some justification for keeping them as long as that income was given to the poor. But that seems highly doubtful.

Would Christianity's founder—Christ—live in the Vatican? Would he walk through the Vatican museum amidst all the gold and jewels and silver and not think of giving them to the starving and sick? It is hard to see how he could do this. Yet, that is what our popes do every day. It makes us wonder when humans will ever become human.

Maybe our fundamental lack as humans today is a lack of heart. We have brilliant scientists, brilliant thinkers, but we can only think what our heart tells us. A truly human heart would never let its intellectual brilliance build an atomic bomb. A truly human heart does not seek to amass untold wealth while billions live in squalid poverty. A truly human heart does not seek to divide but to embrace. A truly human heart seeks to love, not to destroy.

A lack of heart creates a world both on an individual and collective basis where hatred skews and deforms our humanity. The truly great people in history had heart—Gandhi, Martin Luther King, Christ, the Buddha. We need a Ph.D. of the heart more than that of the mind. If the heart is off track, so will the world.

How do we produce a world where people have heart? Part of the answer is that we have it already. There are many with great, kind hearts. What is needed is leadership to meld all those hearts into a force that will reshape the world with kindness and love. Only then can the healing process for all of humanity begin. That takes us to our next major topic—politics.

CHAPTER 3

POLITICS

We do not live alone in the world. There are others. There are 7 billion of us now. And that raises the question of how we are to organize our lives together. That is what politics is all about. How do we allocate power, if we allocate it at all? What is the decision-making process?

The current mantra is democracy—rule by the people. It sounds good, but how does it work in practice? As the U.S. claims that it is the most democratic country in the world, that maybe a good place to start.

Unfortunately, the view is very, very depressing. Yes, once every few years, people can fill out a ballot and vote for a candidate. But that candidate is there largely as a result of money. He or she who can raise a lot of money—or has a lot of money—gets on the ballot.

And where does that money come from? Those who have the money. And who are those who have the money? Certainly not the ordinary citizen, but the rich and powerful. So, whose interests are the elected officials going to represent? Those who gave them the money.

Yes, they will play a game before the cameras, but when push comes to shove, they know who buttered their bread.

As a result, 99% of Americans have to make do with only half of the national wealth. Cities are full of slums, people cannot get health care, inner city schools are decrepit, and yet they are all taught to believe that this is the greatest nation on earth. Listening to any politician is painful in the extreme. You know that you cannot trust half of what they say. Their analysis of problems sickens the listening mind

In 2010, two thirds of the U.S. Senate were millionaires. The average net worth of a member of the House of Representatives was $666,000. The average American's net worth is only one fifth of that. It would be more accurate to say that the U.S. is a moneyocracy or a lobbyocracy—rule by the lobbyists. Whichever label one chooses, U.S. democracy is a materialistic democracy—a product of the materialistic mindset that originates in the late middle ages.

But there is another type of democracy, though its author, Plato, does not think of it as a democracy. That is the rule by the wise.

The wise ruler knows the form of the good, the highest of all the forms. Because it is the highest form, it is not fully explicable in terms of the lower forms. Yet, we get a sense of what it is. The wise ruler will provide for the satisfactory needs of everybody—such as food, clothing, shelter, education, health care.

But the wise ruler will do more. He or she (and Plato recognized that a woman could be a ruler) will make sure that the entire cultural life of the citizens will conform to the form of the good—listening to good music, enjoying good art, interacting peacefully with each other, making sure that feelings conform to reason.

How does the wise ruler learn all these things?

Plato, in his Republic, makes a suggestion. He says we must watch children from when they are very young. If they exhibit signs of leadership, then we should keep a special eye on them. Of course, if they exhibit bad tendencies like bullying or stealing other kids' lunches, they will not be selected to advance further.

Those who meet these stringent standards will be enrolled at the age of 8 in a rigorous course of education which lasts 12 years. It will be heavily influenced by mathematics, as it is essential for a society's leaders to have a disciplined mind.

At the age of 20, if they have not exhibited any bad tendencies, they are sent out for 20 years to gain practical experience in governing. They will begin with small tasks, but as they prove themselves, they will be assigned ones with greater responsibilities.

Finally, after navigating through all these tasks, they will be brought back in at the age of 40 to begin the final and most serious part of their training—the study of philosophy. For 12 years, they will wrestle with the fundamental questions of life—and death. Only when they have successfully done this for 12 years, will they be allowed at age 52 to address the problems of a nation as its supreme ruler.

Some may ask is this a democracy?

The short answer is yes, because it takes a community to select and train the wise ruler. The ruler will embody the peoples' highest ideals. The ruler will know that justice and equality are essential for a society. A ruler will know peace not war is beneficial for all peoples. A ruler will know the beautiful from the ugly. A ruler will know what is of enduring worth and what is transitory. A ruler will know that integrity and honesty are more important than millions in the bank.

One may ask—is all this possible?

The answer is yes.

For example, once upon a time, there was no system for certifying brain surgeons. Yet we came up with one. Likewise, the same can be done with politics.

Of course, it will not be easy—in fact it will be much, much harder. But people have wanted from time immemorial just and wise rulers, but have been prevented from achieving that by the greedy, violent and avaricious. It is true that the people have to handle and contain the greedy, violent and avaricious while this transformation of society takes place. But gradually the latter too will be healed when they begin to see the benefits of living in peace and joy.

The single most important element in training the future leaders is the shaping of their hearts to be kind, generous, unselfish. Plato would not allow his leaders to own private property so that they could not be corrupted. The people would provide for them—adequately but not sumptuously.

Now, how all this is going to be implemented on a practical basis is not easy. It presumes that there is a reservoir of people who are already kind, generous and unselfish. It is implicit in Plato's thought that there are such people.

Are there such people?

The simple answer is yes. One of the great tragedies so far of human history is that the vast reservoir of goodness and kindness that exists in people has not been tapped to lead the world. The pessimist in us will say that it will never happen. Of course, if one says that, it becomes a self-fulfilling prophecy.

But pessimism is the hallmark of the materialistic person. Hope and optimism have their roots in that part of us that transcends and is deeper than the physical world. A true ruler recognizes that each human being has an intrinsic dignity that can never be impinged on. A true ruler recognizes that the resources of the earth are to be utilized to provide adequate food, clothing, housing, education and health care for all. A true ruler recognizes that there must be freedom so that the talents of all may contribute to the human good.

How can we produce good rulers?

This is not an easy question to answer, and reasonable people can disagree on the specifics. But it is a question that we must address urgently. The current system is haphazard at best, and corrupt at worst.

In the U.S, for example, any citizen can decide to run for any office, even the highest in the land, without any real training or vetting. Of course, there is a minor vetting in terms of whether one has a criminal record, or whether there have been any embarrassing incidents in his or her history. But there is little or no requirement that such a candidate has the requisite moral and intellectual training to justify depositing with them the reins of power to make decisions for their fellow Americans.

The consequences of that lack can be devastating. George W. Bush, for example, launched the Iraq war in 2003 to topple Saddam Hussain. 8 ½ years later, we can now tally up the cost. 4,500 U.S. military personnel killed. 30,000 seriously wounded. Over 160,000 Iraqis killed, more than a million displaced, and a trillion dollars spent in doing so. (Some estimates put the actual cost in the two-three trillion dollar range.) Even if it were justifiable and laudable to get rid of Saddam Hussain, was the cost worth it?

Desire for power is the ultimate temptation for humans. People will sacrifice everything else that is dear to them for power. As a consequence, the true ruler has to be somebody who does not want power, but somebody who wants the best for the people that he/she is entrusted with. Clearly, this takes years of discipline and training, and many will be weeded out along the way. But it is essential if a society is to have a ruler that is not intoxicated by power. To help in this process, Plato's suggestion that a ruler not be allowed to own any private property seems to be a good idea,

So, moral training in all its dimensions is the first prerequisite for any ruler—utter honesty, complete incorruptibility, wisdom, impartiality, integrity. The heart of this training is the recognition that each human being is of inestimable worth—in Kant's words, an end in itself, an entity without price. If all realized this and implemented it, there would be no dictators, greed merchants, or anybody who would prey on anybody else. Whether one is fat, ugly, stupid, or beautiful and intelligent makes no difference. All are human beings with a right to be treated equally. The vast majority of humanity's problems would be eliminated or drastically reduced in one fell swoop if this principle was abided by. It would ensure that our policy decisions were wise and to the benefit of mankind. It is the most fundamental principle to be taught to all, especially to those who will rule.

The task, obviously, is monumental. Whether anybody is able to scale the heights of such perfection is, of course, uncertain, but that is no reason to abandon such an ideal. Even a partial attainment is better than our current situation.

And the training has to begin at an early age. Of course, this is a training that has to be given to all children, and this raises the question of how we perceive that somebody has leadership potential. Despite all the research by psycho-biologists and others, this still seems to be very much an intuitive judgment. That is not necessarily wrong, and if more precise methods develop in the sciences, they will be a welcome addition. But we must all remember that morality is not reducible to science.

The second component is intellectual ability. Of course, this can never be divorced from morality, but a future leader needs to be rigorously grounded in a knowledge of history, political science, economics, science and—above all—philosophy, for philosophy is that which pulls all the other disciplines together. The higher the office, the deeper the grounding.

How all of this is to be implemented and who will do it, are, of course, complex questions to be worked out. But the great difficulty can never justify doing nothing. Mankind cannot continue on its present course of having leaders who are beholden to the few and ignorant of the fundamental truths. That is a recipe for disaster.

It may well be that special institutions have to be established to help accomplish these goals. The cost will be far less than the cost of the opposite. The cost of the Iraq war is but one small example.

CHAPTER 4

GOD AND RELIGION

At no time in history have questions about God and religion been so fierce. Given the materialistic mindset that has shaped our modern world, that is not surprising. But it is also not surprising for another reason. Some of those who held themselves out as leaders of churches and religions exhibited such venality that they repelled many good people from questions about God. But any discussion of God and religion must abstract from those historical abnormalities and atrocities.

We must also not let the anthropomorphisms of humanity cloud our vision. Anthropomorphisms are natural and at times helpful, but they can also impede our thinking on these issues. The notion of an elderly man with a long beard sitting on a throne somewhere in the sky may give concrete expression to a belief, but we cannot confuse the expression with the ultimate reality. It maybe comforting to think of a kindly father watching over us, but may not accord with reality.

So what are the fundamental questions dealing with a god?

The first one and most important one is one that we have come across before in a different context. It ultimately boils down to the nature of reality. Is it just physical or is it also something more?

As scientists delve deeper and deeper into the nature of the physical world, the mystery deepens. Up until 1964, scientists thought atoms were made of electrons, protons, neutrons. But the development of accelerators—colliders—in the 1960's where particles were hurled at fantastic speeds against each other, revealed even smaller particles. The theory of quarks was born. But it would be another 11 years—in 1975—before a quark was detected experimentally.

So, are quarks the end of the story? No. We now have anti-quarks, anti-protons, anti-electrons, anti-neutrons, and a whole host of other particles. Some now think that leptons and quarks are the ultimate constituents of matter. Others are beginning to think that matter is ultimately made up of mathematical equations—which of course are not material entities.

Some scientists are arguing that there may be multiverses, instead of a universe. Many physicists posit that there must be dark matter out there in order to explain what is going on. Our universe has increased its rate of expansion instead of slowing down. Will it ever stop? The inner structure of matter is becoming increasingly less comprehensible.

Will science ever come to an ultimate answer, will it ever say that it now knows everything and close its books? Of course, that will never happen because then there will be no more research grants! But on a more serious note, Plato would say that it can never happen because all knowledge about physical things is not knowledge but theory, that can change from one time to another. Scientists admit that nothing is 100% certain in science.

The materialist thus has to admit that he or she does not know what matter is. They may have theories about it, but they do not know what it is. Hence, when the materialist claims that reality is only matter, the materialist does not know what he or she is claiming because they do not know what matter is—and never will. That is a very uncomfortable position to be in. Does the materialist have a defense?

The only defense that the materialist has is to throw the same charge back at the non-materialist—namely that the non-materialist does not know what this non-material dimension of reality is.

However, there are at least 2 crucial differences.

First, unlike matter, there are no layers of reality to roll back with respect to the non-material. While we may progress in plumbing its depths, still it is of one warp and woof. Matter is different. We find a particle, and then discover that it is made of smaller particles, and then of smaller particles etc. That becomes a never-ending quest. Matter is like a will-o-the-wisp. One moment you see it. Then in the next instance, it is gone.

Second, the materialist admits that he or she does not have certainty about any scientific claim. Today's "truth" could be on the scrap heap tomorrow. The non-materialist is not in that position. For example, do you want to claim that child molestation or rape is not wrong, or that you are not certain about it? You have more certainty about this than does the most brilliant scientist regarding the nature of matter. In other words, contrary to popular opinion, there is certainty in at least one area—ethics, whereas there is none in science at all. This fundamental truth challenges much of contemporary thinking, where to label something as scientific is to grant it the badge of certainty. But science is never certain. It is always tentative.

In other words, there are moral laws in reality, and moral laws are not the types of things that you can put under a microscope or in a petri dish. Were moral laws created by the Big Bang?

One may attempt to explain moral laws away by characterizing them as taboos placed by previous societies. Even if that were so and even if the nature of a taboo was adequately explained, that does not help the materialist. If those societies did it, they did it for a reason, and that reason was that it was wrong.

So, if reality has an ethical dimension that is non-material, are there possibly other dimensions?

One of the outstanding and astonishing achievements of modern science is to show the incredible intricacies of the material world. For example, one estimate claims that the human brain has 100 billion neurons and 100 trillion synapses. Chance? If that was the case, Las Vegas would have been out of business a long time ago.

In other words, there also seems to be some ordering dimension to reality. Whether it is an anthropomorphism to claim that this is a person is really an irrelevant question. Our brains are the way they are, not by some incredibly lucky chance action in evolution, but because there is some sort of ordering principle in reality.

Is that all?

There are several other areas which give us pause for reflection, and we have spoken about these in a different context. There is good in the universe. However one defines that goodness, it is there. From the balloon pilot who gave his life to save his passengers to the magnificent sacrifice of the priest in the concentration camp referred to above, there are abundant examples of goodness every day. There is kindness in the universe. Some people are genuinely kind to others.

Can we explain this by some quark or lepton, some chance concatenation of subatomic particles? Are quarks and leptons other-regarding? Putting it in simple terms, would one quark die for another?

That simply does not seem plausible and does not jive with our experience. Such acts of goodness and kindness are done freely, and subatomic particles do not seem to possess freedom. An old principle states that something cannot be in the effect without being in the antecedent cause. In other word, if some people are good and kind, what must be in the nature of the universe from which they came?

All this should give us pause for some profound reflection. If reality has these dimensions, what is the significance of that.? Such reflections may be the beginning of wisdom, and surely this world needs a little more wisdom.

It is one of the great contributions of religious traditions such as Hinduism, Buddhism, Judaism, Christianity and Islam that this physical world in which we live, breathe and have our being, is not the fullness of reality—that reality is far more deep and profound, that there is more than what meets the eye. This realization is liberating. Without that realization, we are shackled to the here and now. With that realization, we are lifted beyond the here and now. This realization does not deny the reality of the here and now. In fact, it enables us to see the here and now in its greater beauty, as that which leads us to an even deeper appreciation of how wonderful reality is. Everybody has been entranced by the beauty of a sunset or the magnificence of that creation which we call a tree. And are we entranced because those physical manifestations are leading us to those fuller depths of reality?

So, we are blessed to live in such a wonderful universe—we who inhabit this amazing little planet on the outer reaches of the universe. Yes, once upon a time before Copernicus, we thought that we were the center of the universe. His discoveries shattered that belief. But contrary to the belief of some that this somehow belittled man, in fact it made us realize that we are part of an incredible thing called the universe. As scientists discover more and more about it, our wonder grows greater and greater in the realization that we two-legged creatures are engaged in an incredible experience here on this little piece of rock.

And when we think of all the things that came together to make life possible here on this planet, was it sheer chance, luck or something else? In our calmer, wiser moments, we may think that it was something else.

What is this something? Each religion has sought to instantiate it in its own unique way. There is nothing inherently wrong with this if we always remember that each such instantiation is a product of a particular culture, and that as no cup can hold the entire ocean, so no culture can be the full and complete expression of something that is infinitely vast and profound.

Judaism (and Christianity) talk of God walking with Adam and Eve in the cool of the evening in the Garden of Eden. A wonderful image denoting the love and concern of a deity for mankind. Did God actually walk with them? The answer is irrelevant. What is important is the message. Man is not alone here in the universe. This entity that is at the heart of reality cares for us.

Some may decry this as pie in the sky, as seeking comfort and consolation in a cold and heartless universe. This hard-headed realism is good, but if it is true to itself, it must also recognize—as we saw earlier—that there is goodness in reality. Where does this goodness come from? The only conclusion is that it is woven into the fabric of reality, and we should be humbled and eternally grateful for that. The world would be a very different place if it were not there.

For all their faults in practice—and they are legion—many of the religious traditions of the world are a great source of hope for humanity. If they could avoid getting into internecine conflicts with each other, they would avoid violating their own fundamental principles. Hinduism best expresses this multi-lateral approach when it says that there are many paths to the top of the mountain.

The decline of religion in the world is but another manifestation of the creeping influence of the materialist mindset. This mindset inevitably involves a diminution of hope. So the more it gains hold, the more the tentacles of despair make their way into the human heart. And without hope, a person cannot live. We know that one of the characteristics of mental illness is a lack of hope. Couple this lack with the awesome destructive power embedded in nuclear weapons, and we have a recipe for the ultimate catastrophe.

So our generation needs to think again about the question of God—whether on a walk under a star-filled sky at night or in a shopping mall. That there is such an entity seems logically irrefutable, and if so, that behooves us to live always under that awareness. It should guide our actions in everything we do. However a particular culture instantiates that entity—while important—is not the most important thing.

That awareness is liberating. It means that we are not bound by the buildings and concrete and contraptions of modern life. Maybe that is why we feel a sense of peace and oneness when we walk by the ocean or through a canopy of trees. For these things were not made by us, but some other entity, and their very beauty and genuineness speak to us in a very direct and immediate way. We are indeed fortunate that we have the gift and privilege of life to enjoy and experience such wonderful things.

This brings us to a topic both of profound concern to us all, and one that, upon reflection, we can see to be one of the greatest of gifts that we have been given—love and sex.

CHAPTER 5

LOVE AND SEX

There is no topic harder to write about than love and sex because it affects us all so intimately. Yet it is one that needs to be written about.

Somebody said some time ago that there has probably been no other country that has had so much sex as the U.S, and yet is so unhappy. Whether this factually true or not, I do not know, but if true, it makes consistent sense.

Sex as we all know is the greatest of all human pleasures. At its best and greatest, it transports us for a brief period out of this world.

But it also brings us back. Without the ingredient of love, it cannot bring us happiness. Momentary pleasure, yes. Lasting happiness, no.

So what is love?

One of the hardest tasks is to separate the essential from the non-essential regarding love. Especially in the beginning when everything seems to be sunshine and flowers, that differentiation is not always easy to make. Maybe an example will help.

They have just gotten married. She is young and beautiful. He is young and handsome. They have just looked into each other's eyes and said that they will love each other and be faithful to each other in sickness or in health, for better or worse, until death do them part.

They are driving away after the reception with the Just Married sign hanging in the rear window—when they come to the first intersection, and lo and behold, a ten ton semi smashes into the side of the car. She is critically injured. She will never be able to have sex again.

What does he do? Here he is, a virile young man with a strong sex drive. Does he say to her "You know how it is, I love you, but I am a young man and - - - - - - -!" Would real love say that, or would real love say "I promised you until death do us part", and remain faithful to her?

We may try to wriggle out of this one, but at the end of the day, we have to confront the issue head on. Difficult as it may be, I think we have to say that true love requires that he remain faithful to her. I have a personal example that confirms this.

Approximately 30 years ago, the young wife of a friend of mine went into hospital for brain surgery. In the process, the surgeon made a mistake that caused her to be paralyzed for life. Every day he bathed her and fed her. and never once did he stray outside his marriage vows. She died a few years ago. There is a nobility on his face today that gives the answer better than any words ever can.

The reality is that love is primarily, but not exclusively, something non-physical, non-material. It is a commitment to another person—not just to a body. It is the giving of the fullness of your being to another, and we know that the fullness of that being is more than the body—it is the total self. It transcends time, and is willing to die for the other if need be.

There is a damaged submarine on the ocean floor. The escape hatch will only allow one person to escape. There are two people in it. If you really love the other person, would you say something like "Well, this hurts me more than it hurts you, but you know how it is - - - - - - -", and as you disappear into the escape hatch. you turn and say "Have a nice day"—or better, "Have a nice eternity"?

We all hope, of course, that we never have to face such situations, but when you say that you love somebody, you have to mean in your heart that you would sacrifice your life for that other person, or refrain from sex with anybody else if your spouse for some reason cannot have sex.

Such are the demands of love.

And yet for those who genuinely love, the rewards are beyond words. There is a peace and happiness and joy that transcends this earthly realm.

Sex can be creative and destructive. Not only can sex create a child, but sex united with love can produce the profoundest of human relationships. Without it, sex is like a river without banks. It can flood and destroy. But if it is contained within the bonds of love, the river can be a source of great good.

It is a measure of how far the materialistic mindset has permeated into the modern mind that these concepts are barely ever considered. And the results are staggering and tragic.

By 2004, 35.7% of births in the U.S. were to unmarried women. Swedish researchers documented that children raised by single parents are twice as likely to suffer from psychiatric problems, suicide and other injuries as those raised in intact two-parent homes.

These are statistics but they are about real lives, real children. Is the fragile fabric of our society being gradually torn asunder? As the vast majority of Americans have sex without being in a committed relationship, is this having an adverse effect on the structure of American life?

A recent study by the U.S. Centers for Disease Control and Prevention (CDC) sends a chilling warning. It claims that 60% of Americans say that as children, they had abusive or troubled family members or parents, who were absent due to divorce or separation. These experiences included physical or sexual abuse, domestic violence, drug or alcohol abuse. More than 1 in 10 claimed sexual abuse. One of the authors of the report, Valerie Edwards, said that the actual figures may be higher, as there is a tendency to underreport such things. The findings are published in the December 17, 2010 issue of CDC's "Morbidity and Mortality Weekly Report".

These childhood experiences are associated with greater instances of depression, cancer, diabetes, heart disease, and premature death. 29% of the respondents in the survey reported that they grew up in homes where there was drug or alcohol abuse. A recent report, America's Children: Key National Indicators of Well-Being 2011, states that drug use among 8th graders increased from 8% in 2009 to 10% in 2010.

This terrifying picture can lead one to conclude that America's biggest enemy is not without, but within. Al-Quaeda and similar groups could save their resources and simply wait for the U.S. to collapse from within. It is akin to a building riddled with termites, who are eating away at its fundamental structure. One day, the entire structure will collapse.

Numerous sociological studies document this decay. Why? For one simple but profound reason.

Happiness is primarily and fundamentally a non-material entity. It is a state of mind that is not fleeting like pleasure. We can only take so much pleasure before physiologically the senses are saturated and dulled. Happiness can be endless, and happiness does not just happen. It requires putting a primacy on our non-physical self, even if at times that requires a possible denial of the physical self.

That is part of the fundamental human endeavor. To be human is to be more than an animal. That which make us human and thus more than an animal may, at times, require discipline, self-control. As the arrow can never hope to reach its target unless the archer disciplines the bow to propel it properly, so it is likewise with humans in the area of sexuality and love. Happiness can only be achieved when both are married together. Their separation in contemporary American life is but one manifestation of the malaise of unhappiness that exists in the American psyche.

Someone asked a short time ago if anybody had seen a truly happy American recently. There was silence in the room. Materialism in whatever form it takes can never produce happiness. Matter is the realm of the ephemeral, the transitory. Happiness does not lie in those kingdoms. Happiness can only come from another and deeper source in the human spirit. Unless sexual activity is guided by genuine love, it can never bring us to the promised land that we all desire—real happiness. Sex that is not anchored in love has the capacity to do great harm—devastated hearts, unwanted children, a sense of emptiness and meaninglessness, as if there was no purpose to life. These feelings can be deadly.

Some contemporary so-called sex therapists such as Ian Kerner—who has a Ph.D.—see nothing really wrong in casual sex. Once again, the materialistic mindset distorts reality. The fact is that the physical dimension of sex is the springboard to something more than the physical—to love. Cut off from love, sex is a wasteland of the human spirit, and all who venture there will reap the results of that wasteland. It will be a lonely walk in a desert. Sex without genuine love can never bring real happiness.

But where sex is joined with genuine love, and two people are fused in one mentally, emotionally, spiritually as well as physically, it is one of the greatest joys on earth, and provides the strongest bulwark when challenges arise from life.

In its Declaration of Independence, Americans vowed that everybody has the right to life, liberty and the pursuit of happiness. With sex, that pursuit is not possible without love.

This theme once again reinforces the conviction that the materialistic mindset is eating away at the core of humanity. Our ancestors wrestled with this greatest question of all—what is the nature of reality—and concluded that there was more to it than met the eye. Their instantiation of this belief may have been limited and in many cases flawed, but at least they held onto that core insight.

Today in the West, one area where this materialistic mindset regarding sex is most visible is in the semi-nude, nude and pornographic images—especially of women—that flood the world. This utilization of the natural beauty of a human body to sell everything from cars to soap—and to titillate—is a manifestation of a mindset that is ultimately destructive. The Moslem world to its credit recognizes this, and while in many Moslem countries, this goes too far by forcing women to wear burkhas, nevertheless it makes a point. Also, of course, it is well known that when some Moslem men get outside of their countries, they engage in sex acts which would never be tolerated at home. But, at least, many Moslems still adhere to standards that used to prevail in the West before materialism took over. In the pre-materialistic days, it was recognized that a person was more than his or her body.

This materialistic conception of sex is driven in significant part—to put it mildly—by money. In the process, it not only degrades those with beautiful bodies by making them into objects, not people, but it also degrades those who are not aesthetically endowed. Our society immediately puts them into a second or third class status because of their looks. Not only is this not wise, but it is an affront to human dignity

For the last 300-400 years, that core insight of previous times has been gradually eroded away. The people who caused the erosion, may have been well-intentioned, but that does not make them right. If this belief ever fully takes hold—or gets even close to it—the potential disaster for humanity is beyond words. As noted earlier, we now possess enough nuclear weapons to destroy this planet 100 times over. People who are genuinely happy do not destroy this planet.

"Who would be so mad as to do that?" you might ask. We know on an individual basis that people do those things when everything seems black and bleak. So, it is likewise on a collective basis. The 20th. century saw two devastating world wars. Those are warning signs of disaster lurking on the horizon. The good (and bad) news is that there will be only one more world war—for there will be nothing left after it.

To avoid such a catastrophe, we (especially in the West) need to confront that ultimate question about the nature of reality in all areas of our lives. We need to triumphantly affirm that reality is more than the bricks and stones that we see. If we do, we will once again re-introduce hope into humanity. When genuine love is conjoined with sex, humanity will be happy. We will once again be able to produce not just happy children, but also works of art that ennoble the human spirit, not ignoble it.

CHAPTER 6

ART

In every age, art has provided a window into the soul. Coming as it does from the depths of the human spirit—and in the case of great art—either unfiltered by the restrictions of the conscious mind or fused seamlessly with it—it speaks to us with an immediacy that can be gripping and powerful. What does "modern" art tell us today?

Among many in the public, the term "modern art" provokes a confused, at times despising, response. When they "hear" the "silent concerto", when they see "paintings" by elephants wielding a paint brush, when they see penknives as major exhibits in art galleries, some are tempted to ask "is this art?"

Others, of course, see modern art as being great art, as breaking new frontiers, as articulating the spirit of the new age that is upon us. But just because something breaks a new frontier, does not mean that it is great art.

Who is right, if any?

In order to make overarching sense of what is happening in art, we need to remember the profound change that has taken place in the thinking of humanity in the last 300-400 years. Many at the heights of Western culture have seriously questioned the world view of the previous 2000 years in the West—which for purposes of being succinct and brief, we have referred to as the view of Plato.

The greatest fusion of the material and more-than-material probably was achieved in Greek sculpture and by some of the Renaissance painters such as Michelangelo and Rembrandt. The Middle Ages had virtually eliminated the material from its paintings. Bodies were lifeless entities covered by cloth, often with a halo around their head. But they were not human.

With the Renaissance, bodies became bodies again, but they were imbued with a humanity that reaches across the centuries to us today. Almost any face of the figures in the Sistine Chapel touches us with its humanity. The ability of great art is that it touches the core of our being, its physical representation sending us a transcendent message, which we can digest endlessly, but never entirely put into words. And that transcendent message comes to us whole, not analytically dissected until it is lifeless and desiccated. True art transmits life in all its profundity, and captivates our total being.

Does modern art captivate our total being? Do the fractured bodies of a Picasso do this?

The sad answer seems to be no. Rather, they reflect the fractured spirit which is the modern soul, often tortured, never complete, never whole.

The modern symphony repels, pushes the listener away. A Beethoven symphony engages the heart, mind and soul of the listener.

All of this stems from the materialism that has seeped into the soul of modern man. For the first time in recorded history, materialism has become the dominant culture, and it will wreak havoc on the great achievements of the past.

In contrast, Beethoven's great 5th. Symphony engages the very depths of the listener. The notes take one through a catharsis from despair to hope. Modern classical music by and large distances itself from the listener, as do modern paintings and sculpture. That is what materialism does. As in the economic sphere with capitalism which is engrossed solely with the individual, so likewise, much of modern art in all its forms is locked into an individualism that locks out the rest of us. To touch another, one cannot be imprisoned by the barricades of individualism,

It was presaged with Martin Luther when he stood there before the Diet of Worms, and said "Here I stand, I can do no other." Yes, he was fighting corruption on a horrendous scale and we feel great sympathy for him, but he was also casting off his fellow human beings and striking out on his own. He was leaving the lifeboat, and we know what lies outside the lifeboat.

Genuine humanity means never totally casting off another human being, no matter how twisted and contorted the latter may be. One may never be able to undo the damage that has been done to a human being, but one can never do the even greater damage of casting them off completely.

The recent documentary "Buck" is a brilliant and heart-warming depiction of humanity. Cruelly beaten by his father as a child, Buck grows up to be a horse trainer who is able to communicate his humanity and integrity to horses, who respond in amazing fashion.

Sadly, so much of a modern art is soulless. But that is what you get in a materialist culture. Will art ever regain its soul? Not unless it rejects the materialistic philosophy that propels so much of it. One cannot see that inherent dignity that lies in each human face if one's mind does not see the person—that mysterious and wonderful reality that we know exists in each of us.

This is the defining issue of our time, the mental, emotional, spiritual issue that characterizes who we are. Are there still among us enough to reverse the disastrous tide of the last 400 years?

All the great achievements of the recent past—the Universal Declaration of Human Rights, Gandhi, Nelson Mandela, Martin Luther King, Mother Teresa—all these were possible because of the triumph of the human spirit over the merely mundane and pragmatic. Will art once again assume that mantle to lift up the human spirit? That is one of the great questions of our time. If we regain our belief in the dignity of each human being, the answer is yes. If we do not regain this, the answer is no.

CHAPTER 7

EDUCATION

Everybody agrees that education is important.

But there is a gaping hole at its very heart.

There is unanimity of thought that students should be prepared for the technological society that we live in—that students be well educated in math, science, writing etc. Our modern society could not function unless there were well trained workers.

The overwhelming emphasis in our current educational system is to prepare people for the material dimension of our existence. In the 19th century, Americans developed its public schools to prepare its children for the booming commercial economy. At the turn of the 20th century, high schools were deemed necessary to give those students additional training. The same then occurred for colleges and universities, and received a major boost under the GI bill after World War 2, to prepare returning veterans for the market place. Math, science and English were regarded as being the most important subjects. Yes, they are very important, but are they the most important?

Today, South Korea embodies those commercial values probably more than anybody else. The pressure is most keen in high school because in November each year, seniors take the all-important exam which will determine their future. To prepare them for it, parents can spend $1,000 a month for after-school tutoring, which can go on till midnight. The government recently passed a bill requiring these institutions to stop at 10p.m. The pressure is so great that in one survey, a fifth of middle and high school students felt tempted to commit suicide. Sadly, 15 out of every 100,000 do so. The system stresses excessively rote learning over thinking. As one student put it, "We are like memorizing machines." Seoul may be the name of its capital, but it has very little soul.

But a human being is not simply a worker, not just a cog in the material dimension of our existence. A human being is a person of great feeling, a person who loves, a person who interacts with other human beings who have similar dimensions. Human beings grow, then face the reality of advancing age. Human beings live in societies where decisions are made about the allocation of scarce human resources. Human beings are people who face the mystery of their own being, the mystery of other human beings, the mystery of the universe. Human beings face the question of the meaning of life, the meaning of everything.

A student could be brilliant in math and science, but what if the student is not kind, honest, just, hard-working, caring? Which is better—a whiz in math and science, but unkind, dishonest, unjust and uncaring—or a person who is deficient in math, science and English, but kind, honest, just, hardworking and caring?

I know that we would like to say that the ideal is one who is good in math and English, and also kind, honest, just, hardworking and caring. We hope that this ideal is the norm, but if we had to make a choice, which one would we choose? That choice is very instructive. At the end of the day, if we had to make that choice, we would have to say that the latter is more important than the former.

But, one might ask, how do you train somebody to be kind, honest, just, hardworking and caring? Isn't that up to the individual—a product of genetics? Isn't that a matter of individual choice?

Of course, history shapes us all powerfully. Cruelty inflicted on an ancestor could well have some physiological and psychological effect on succeeding generations. That makes the human task harder but not impossible.

An interesting and instructive example of that is shown, as mentioned above, in the recent documentary "Buck". It is the true story of a boy who was beaten mercilessly when he was young, but grows up not only to be a horse trainer who has an incredible way with horses, but also a human being of great wisdom, compassion, humor and humanity.

It is this dimension of our educational system that is most lacking. Of course, parents and other family members play the primary role in the shaping of a child's character. But as the material dimension of our existence has created the need for an outside educational system because parents simply cannot be masters of the complexities of physics, chemistry, biology, math, history, psychology etc., so we have to deal with the role that teachers must play in the shaping of children's characters.

2,500 years ago, Confucius preached that if we could only instill the right habits in children from an early age, we would have little or no need for laws etc., because these children would do the right thing as they grew up. Obviously, that has never become a widespread practice, but that is no reason to stop trying.

Another objection is that ethics is up to the individual. If one means by this that a person has the freedom to choose whether to do the right thing or the wrong thing, that is obviously true. We have the gift of freedom.

But if somebody means that it is the individual who is the determiner of what is right and wrong, then this cannot withstand critical analysis. This is Ethical Subjectivism. If an individual determines that cruelty is ethical, can that possibly be true?

Now, it is true that there are times when it is not easy to determine what is the kind thing to do. We say that sometimes one has to be cruel to be kind. What that means is that the recipient may view it as cruel, but the intention of the other party is to be kind. The child may think that you are the most cruel person in the world if you stop him or her from gorging on a whole box of Twix bars, but that is not cruelty, it is kindness.

But if one were to advocate the position that mercilessly beating, then carving up a child is ethical if the perpetrator thinks it is, then that is clearly ludicrous—and seriously dangerous. And yet, this ethical subjectivism is abroad in the land.

If there is a set of ethical standards and values that all human beings should follow, the question then becomes how to inculcate these into young children so that these values become second nature to them. The natural objection is how we do find people in whom these values are already inculcated.

Yes, this is indeed a problem, and is similar to the one we found in Politics—how do you find people to train future leaders?

And yet again, if we do not start some place, we will never start at all. It is better to have an imperfect start, rather than no start at all.

Fortunately, there are people out there who embody those central values. They may not be perfect, but the human odyssey is one of continually striving to be better and better. These people have to be the foundation on which we build a better future.

While financial compensation can never be the ultimate arbiter of worth, a case can be made that teachers should be compensated more than any other group, because they are the ones who are so powerfully shaping the future of the world. Certainly, they should be paid more than the financial gurus of Wall Street. A strong case can be made that they should be paid more than doctors. While the latter have a very important place in life, and at times a critical place, nevertheless, the teacher spends infinitely more time with a student than does a doctor. The daily interaction that shapes the student's values and feelings clearly dwarfs the rare visit to a doctor. The latter is primarily concerned with the physical body. The former deals with that which is central to our existence—our spirit.

Of course, we know the economic worth that contemporary U.S. society places on teachers. They make only a fraction of what bankers, lawyers and doctors make. Is it any wonder then that the U.S. has such a poor education system? What a difference there would be if every teacher was rigorously trained and screened, and devoted their whole selves to their task! Finland has just such a system. A teacher has a higher social status than a doctor. And Finland has one of the best education systems in the world—if not the best.

From a purely economic perspective, our society would save untold billions by paying teachers well, because of a reduction in crime. Currently, the U.S. has more people in prison—on an absolute basis—than any other country in the world. Some estimates claim that a full 5% of the U.S. population is either in prison or on probation at any given time. When one also factors in the money spent on crime prevention and rehabilitation programs, the cost is staggering. Ethics is cost effective!

Those entrusted with inculcating those central values of kindness, honesty, justice, hard work and caring should embody those values. In other words, they cannot be simply abstractions for them. Children must see that their teachers are kind, honest, just, hardworking and caring. Example is the best teacher.

Some may legitimately question whether such values can be taught. They may say that you either have those values or you do not. Yet, consider the influence that technology is having on children today. Computers, I-Pads, I-Pods and everything in between are clearly shaping the contemporary child. If technology can do that, why not example?

The objection may arise from the materialistic mindset that blankets so much of modern thought that this is impossible. But people like Plato believed that the mind—reason—should govern our feelings. Hume, probably the single greatest exponent of the materialistic mindset, said that reason is and should always be the slave of the passions. In a nutshell, that is the watershed in modern thought from a view that there is something more than the material, to the view that everything is ultimately matter.

The ideal, of course, is when reason and feeling go hand in hand. That is beautiful to behold. But in those cases where feeling is not in complete harmony with reason, that is where the discipline of reason must prevail until such a time as that harmony is achieved.

The biblical story of Adam and Eve in the garden sums up our human situation. They were told not to eat the fruit of a particular tree, but succumbed because they wanted something. Feeling trumped reason. The rest is history.

But humans can choose reason when there is a disharmony between it and feeling. The alcoholic can say no to that beer. Somebody with an addiction to drugs can say no. Yes, it is hard, very hard at times, but it is possible. There may be many falls on the way, but it is part of our human odyssey to keep getting up.

These are crucial lessons for every child to learn, especially in those early formative years. the Jesuits used to say "Give us a child until 5, and you can have the child for rest of your life." They believed that once that basic formation had taken place, nothing in later life could fundamentally change it. Confucius also believed that those early years were crucial. Install the right habits, and you will not need laws. The multiplicity of our laws indicates how unsuccessful we have been in that task.

Moral education is essential for a successful society. And a true moral education is not a life-denying set of prescriptions. Rather, it is a joyful liberation that unleashes the deepest and best in a human being. It is the recognition that pleasure does not necessarily bring happiness, but that happiness will enable one to enjoy pleasures that bring enduring happiness.

If somebody like a Hitler had received that moral education, how much suffering would have been avoided in the world. The same is true for countless others down through history who brought death and destruction to countless millions, and who do so today. If push came to shove and we had to choose between a technological education and a moral education, the world could be happy without the former, but not the latter. People were happy long before there were I-Phones and I-Pads. The latter if used properly can be an ingredient in human happiness, but they are not essential.

The root meaning of the word "education" is instructive. It comes from the Latin "educere", which means "to lead out". In other words, the heart of education is not pumping into somebody a whole host of facts and figures. Its heart lies in tapping into that goldmine that thinkers like Socrates and Plato believed existed within us. As Socrates so famously said "The unexamined life is not worth living."

When he walked around the streets of Athens—and in those days you could do that without fear of being run over—he would stop one of the movers and shakers in the city and ask them a question such as "what is justice?" or "what is love?" When the respondent gave his or her reply, Socrates would ask a further question, then another and another. While the respondent might never hit the nail on the head, nevertheless at the end of the questioning, there is the feeling that one is closer to the truth than at the beginning. Pericles, the leader of Athens in its most brilliant years and a contemporary of Socrates, was a great orator who could persuade the Athenians on many things. But Socrates' question was—is what Pericles says, true?

Genuine education is built on the belief that there is a tremendous goldmine in each individual. The task of each teacher is to tap into that goldmine and help the student realize what tremendous potential exists in each one. In some cases, that goldmine may be overlain with layers of suffering or abuse or neglect. But the real teacher is the one who is able to pierce all that, and to get the student to realize the tremendous wealth that is within them. This wealth may vary from individual to individual, but both Socrates and Plato believed that the goldmine is there.

Once this is discovered and brought to the light of day, one will have a love of learning which will last them a lifetime. One will find an infinite fascination in everything—whether it be physics or art or history or biology. Without a love of learning, one is not truly human. With it, the world—and the universe—are places of endless fascination.

And this knowledge is primarily valued not because it can be used for something else, but for its own sake. If it can then be used to alleviate suffering and improve the human condition, fine, but learning is loved primarily for its own sake. One wonders how many can truly say this.

But if those who are blessed to be teachers can impart this love of learning to their students, they will help them avoid educational burnout. In today's exacting educational environment, so many burn out from the pressures heaped on them by the demands of a technological society. People come to hate learning because of that, and that is surely a great tragedy. It is only when there is a love of learning that one can experience one of the greatest joys of mankind.

So our educational system needs to be revamped in its entirety. More rigorous training, more and better screening of potential teachers, a re-ordering of our priorities, all these are essential to a well-functioning society. Above all, each generation must pass on the love of learning to the next. They must hand on the torch. That flame can never be allowed to be snuffed out. Is it in danger of that today? Such judgments are hard to make, but caution would lead us to redouble and re-triple our efforts in case it is.

What is without doubt—as in all areas of life—is that a purely materialistic conception of a human being is not only wrong, but also life-destroying

CHAPTER 8

HISTORY

If you are born and raised in Salt Lake City, you will probably be a Mormon. If you are born and raised in Ireland, the chances are that you will be a Catholic. If you are born and raised in India, the odds are that you will be a Hindu.

This is both a strength and a weakness. The strength is that one is given a set of beliefs. In the best case scenario, one is inculcated with all that is beautiful in the tradition into which one is born. The weakness is that one may see all the other traditions as wrong, that ones own tradition is exclusively right.

Of course, it is possible that ones tradition may possess the "ultimate" truth, and that the others are either wrong or incomplete or both. One problem with this is how do you tell that this is the case.

A new problem has emerged in the contemporary world—namely, that one rejects all the traditions of the past and either lives in a world empty of belief (nihilism), or seeks to fashion something completely new.

Numerous problems surround either approach. In the first, life may be seen as meaningless, absurd, irrational—views that surface in atheistic existentialism. In the second, can one claim that ones views have validity beyond ones individual self, and if so, why should anybody else accept your views?

Hence, history presents us with numerous perplexing problems. What are we to make of the ruminations, insights and beliefs of ancestral humanity as it developed? Did they cotton on to something of profound truth for which we should be grateful to them? Is there any way to solve this conundrum?

It is a thesis of this book that there is a way.

That thesis is that it is part of our central humanity to reflect on the central questions of our existence with love, honesty, rigor, and compassion. Socrates expressed it in a different way—the unexamined life is not worth living—but the meaning is the same—that the true worth of a life is not how much money you have, how good looking you are—but how lovingly, honestly, rigorously and compassionately one grapples with the fundamental questions of existence. We are called on today to do the same as our ancestors did before us.

We are blessed that they left beacons to guide us on our way. We do not have to reinvent the wheel. The question is "what IS the wheel?"

The central theme of all of the great traditions of history—whether it be Hinduism, Buddhism, Judaism, Christianity, Islam or any of the others too numerous to mention here—is that the physical world, the world that we see with our eyes and touch with our hands—is not the sum total of reality or even the most important dimension of reality—that there is a non-physical dimension that far transcends in importance the world of the senses. This can be exemplified in the most abstract of terms or in more down-to-earth ways such as "an act of kindness is worth more than a million dollars".

The different traditions may be cloaked in different historical garments, but underneath those garments is a centrality of thought that unites humanity as one. It is one of the enduring human tasks both to be totally absorbed in one or more of these traditions and to simultaneously see beyond the confining historical garb with which they might be clothed.

The richness and beauty of each of these traditions is one of the great gifts of the past to the present. Sadly, in the past and the present, some adherents of some of these traditions have seen fit to engage in actions contrary to the fundamental tenets of their traditions. For example, Christianity preaches love—even of enemies—yet the crusaders slaughtered untold numbers in its name. For too many years, Catholics and Protestants bombed each other in Northern Ireland. Sunni and Shiite are often at each other's throats today, and Hindus have massacred thousands of Muslims in India.

Our materialistic culture today presents a different challenge. It provides no basis for such things as hope, compassion, kindness. If such things are ultimately reducible to the workings of some subatomic particle, the human spirit is condemned to a prison from which it cannot escape. And that, surely, is bad news for humanity.

This materialistic mindset acts as a great prison of the human mind. It is to the great credit of the past that it threw off those shackles, and broke free to breathe the fresh air of the spirit. At times, this may have resulted in imperfect instantiations, but at least it escaped the prison that materialism sought to confine them in.

Most of human history has been a story of dispersal and differentiation. People spread out of East Africa, and migrated to different climes, where the color of their skin might change, their physical appearance be modified, and their beliefs differentiated.

Ironically—but hopefully—technology is enabling us to come back together again—to make contact with our long lost relatives. We can pick up a phone and call anywhere in the world. We can hop on a plane and be anywhere on the planet in 24 hours or so. We have a lot of catching up to do!

But our task is an exhilarating one—exploring the riches of each cultural tradition—in their food, music, dances, art, ways of governing, beliefs, jokes—and so much more.

And we, like previous generations, can express the beauty and truth in each tradition in our own unique way. The world is so multi-faceted that no one generation can give full expression to the depth and power of these central truths. As long as we remain faithful to the core of those traditions, each generation in its literature and music and paintings—and science—can add to all the previous expressions and leave a richer legacy for coming generations—and hopefully stimulate them to even greater heights, as the past stimulated us.

So, we need to embrace history with great love. It will make for a life of endless fascination, and erase the animosities which fear of the different can generate in us. Instead of building arms, we should link arms. As Hinduism says so beautifully—there are many paths to the top of the mountain. Let us not throw rocks at each other on the way up.

CHAPTER 9

SCIENCE AND TECHNOLOGY

The explosion in science and technology is mind boggling. From those beginnings in Miletus (located in modern day Turkey) around 600 B.C. the development is nothing less than phenomenal. It was then that Thales asked the first modern scientific question "What is everything made of?" Before that, the traditional question was "which god did that?" Today at CERN, scientists hurl subatomic particles around at dizzying speeds in a tunnel on the Swiss-French border. They are asking the same question.

Yet, there is a sobering dimension to this as well. The CERN scientists are trying to answer the same question as Thales—what is everything made of? Thales suggested water because it is a liquid, a solid (when it freezes), and air (when it is heated). Today, at incredible expense, scientists are searching for the Higgs boson—the god particle as they call it—which their theories say must exist. On July 4 of this year (2012) they announced that they have probably found it.

Science becomes more bewilderingly complex day by day. Theories such as string theory or the claim that matter is ultimately reducible to mathematical equations not only boggle the mind, but lead to some very profound questions.

One of those key questions is whether there will ever come a day when scientists will close their books and say that they have answered all the questions. As said above, the cynical answer, of course, is no, because then there would be no more research grants!

But that question raises the very profound one about the very nature of knowledge.

Plato, again, claimed that in science we can never have knowledge in the sense of 100%, absolute proof. Everything in science is ultimately theory. Today's certainty is tomorrow's uncertainty. Science never knows anything. It is chasing a will-o-the-wisp. One moment we think we see it, the next we do not.

And where is it leading us?

In the garden of Eden, Adam and Eve were told by God that they could eat from every tree, except the tree of knowledge/ Why? One would have thought that this was a tree that God would want them to eat from. Why did He forbid them to do this?

Knowledge has given us refrigerators, cars, I-Phones, etc. etc. But knowledge has also given us nuclear weapons, that could wipe out every refrigerator, car and I-Phone from planet earth, and reduce this beautiful, verdant planet to barren rock.

And to think that this is a remote possibility goes against the grain of history. In a moment of anger or fear, we can do many irrational things.

If so, then this raises the even deeper perplexity about the nature of the human enterprise. Are we forever barred from finding the ultimate secret of nature? What does this mean? What is the message for us? These questions are enough to cause a gigantic pause.

One thing that jumps out at us is that if we put even just a small fraction of the effort that we put into science, into the moral dimension of our being, things could be very different in the world. So much of modern scientific effort is geared to making life more pleasant, pleasurable and comfortable for those who are well off. But if all the ingenuity that went into making, for example, the I-Phone, had gone into the alleviation of hunger and poverty for the 3 billion people on earth who live on less than $2 a day, would not the world have been a better place?

Yes, the world around us is a tantalizing mystery, but it is no mystery that billions teeter on the brink of starvation and sickness every day. There is no lack of certainty about that, and all our scientific and technological genius should be targeted at that first. To do any less is to be less than human.

All this reminds us once again that a major part of the human enterprise is to recognize the dignity of humanity in each and every person. If we were starving and barely clinging on to existence, would we want science and technology to be focused on producing a better I-Phone or car or T.V. set?

We may attempt to squiggle and squirm out from underneath the logic of this argument, but in our heart of hearts, we know where the truth lies. The depths of the ocean of science can never be fully plumbed by us, but at least we can know that we are using our minds to fulfill our central human purpose, and never let any of fellow human beings suffer from hunger, pain or disease.

Those unconquered frontiers will always keep our feet firmly planted on the ground. It will humble us that we will never know everything, and that the more we know, the more we know how much we do not know. If knowledge is a ratio comparing how much we know with how much we do not know, then we know less today that we did one hundred years ago, because we now know how much more we do not know.

Our quest for knowledge leads us then to the edge of infinity. It is similar, but on a much greater scale, to the experience that millions have had when they stood on the edge of some place like the Grand Canyon, in awe at its majesty. In science, we stand on the edge of the greatest canyon of all, and that sense of awe at its majesty and mystery can only make us more fully human.

Science, then, instead of being at odds with the spiritual and non-physical, lets us touch the hand of the divine. If we re-envision Michelangelo's famous painting in the Sistine Chapel of God reaching out to touch Adam's hand, we could see that it is man reaching out to touch the hand of the divine. Any modern Michelangelo out there?

Ironically, it may be that as we explore the nature of matter, we may come to the conclusion that our concept of matter as being composed solely of brute matter may be fatally flawed. It may be that matter and non-matter are of one warp and woof.

The old dichotomies will thus give way to a more unified vision, where there may be continuity between them, and no ultimate divide. This would accord more with our actual experience of ourselves. We perceive ourselves as a unity, not as two opposing entities.

This unified vision may spill over into other areas. Instead of seeing dichotomies between nations and races, we may see the continuities. After all, we do all come from the same common parents. Just because our outward migration from East Africa put us in different climates and environments, changing our physical appearance and color, that does not mean that the essentials of who we are changed. One may wear a suit and another a flowing robe, but we are all humans under those different clothes.

In other words, reality may be more wonderful and beautiful and fascinating than we think. It may not be just a lifeless, barren desert of subatomic particles whizzing around at incredible speeds. The physical world may be a gateway to something very sublime. If mankind ever forgets this, then mankind may be condemning himself or herself to a prison from which there is no escape, and where there is no hope.

It is the essence of freedom that mankind does not feel that it is in a prison. In the last 300-400 years, much damage has been done to man's psyche, and much needs to be repaired. But that flame of hope has not been completed snuffed out, It is there in the heart of man, and just needs to be nourished and watered by the greatest thing that has been given to us—our minds.

We need a second Renaissance—one founded on a deeper understanding of who we are and the nature of the world. The first

Renaissance—in significant part—was a revolt against the lifelessness of the previous period, which resulted when it sought to conceive of ourselves as disembodied existences.

But our flesh and blood are not just lifeless corpses. The spirt is not completely devoid of matter, and matter is not completely devoid of the spirit. They go hand in glorious hand, and the fullness of life sees them as seamlessly connected entities.

So science that is pursued with the fullness of life can lead to us to the most whole and holiest of experiences. The fullness of life must be seized with both hands and all our heart. To do less is not to live.

Science is a springboard from which to dive into the mystery of existence. Its rigor and hard-headedness help keep our feet anchored on the ground. But there is more to us than our feet, and we should never think otherwise.

One other danger inherent in contemporary science is the notion by some that the purpose of science is to conquer nature. Is this the last frontier of imperialism?

The fact is that we are part of nature. So, are we trying to conquer ourselves?

It is one thing to try to understand the depths of nature and to try to utilize that knowledge to improve human life. It is another to treat nature as some alien object. We have to be attuned to the rhythms of nature both in us and around us. Nature can seemingly be violent at times—red in tooth and claw as the old saying goes. But nature can also be gentle—that soft breeze rustling through leaves, the gentle kitten that cuddles up to us. All of this is part of nature, and we are called on to understand it in its totality.

But some thinkers, such as Michael G. Zey in his article "Man's Evolutionary Path into the Universe (Futurist, vol. 35, May 2001) proclaim that man's function is the "dominionization" not just of this planet, but the entire universe. While we have been given minds to understand, and while we do not know how much our minds can understand, we always have to remember that we are but puny creatures in this vast universe, and should never have the attitude of mind that we must "dominate" this universe. Such attitudes bespeak of disasters of immense magnitude.

CHAPTER 10

PSYCHOLOGY

If any discipline is unique to the 20th. century, it is psychology. It takes many forms, of course, but in the popular mind, it is inescapably associated with trying to solve the unhappiness of people.

This, in and of itself, of course, is significant. Some people, of course, have always experienced unhappiness, some slightly, some greatly. But in the 20th. century, this problem seemed to become more acute.

Historians suggest various factors—urbanization, for example, where people are uprooted from the land where they and their ancestors toiled for countless generations, and thrust into dirty, overcrowded cities of concrete and steel. Another suggestion is affluence. When every day you are scraping for the bare necessities of existence, you do not have time to be unhappy, the argument goes. Likewise, when you are comfortably situated, you begin to have time to think—about yourself, your life, relationships etc.

Our concern here lies in a different but related area—the fundamental conception of what a human being was.

Plato had famously created the tripartite division of the human soul, reason, spirit and desire. Desire was the animal side of us. It was not inherently bad, but it had to be kept within a tight rein. In Plato's simile, the three dimensions were analogous to a chariot drawn by 2 horses, one of which was desire. This was the one that needed the most discipline from the other two dimensions.

Spirit, the second horse was best described as courage. At times, it had to go against desire. For example, if one gave ones life for a cause or another person, one had to discipline the natural desire to live.

The driver of the chariot was reason, part of whose task was to rein in the two horses at times. Reason, for Plato, was of course a non-physical entity

Contrast this with the tripartite division of Sigmund Freud—the id, ego, superego. The id is all our unconscious drives and desires, and governs the ego and superego. It is a materialistic force that does not comport with reason.

So here we see in psychology that split between a previous age which had a non-physical dimension to reality, and the modern age which is out and out materialistic. If psychology is to be the force for good that it can be, then it needs to re-capture that original belief.

So much of modern psychology is a barren wasteland because it is not invigorated by the fresh springs of the human spirit. Until that day comes, so much of it will be unsatisfactory and unhelpful. A materialistic psychology is ultimately a hollow husk masquerading as a life giving force. Psychology needs the re-birth of the human spirit.

CHAPTER 11

DEATH

There is probably no subject that we like to think about less than death. It seems to represent the end of our dreams—no more walks on the beach, no more hours in the arms of a loved one, no waking up to the vibrancy of a spring morning.

And yet we know that it is inevitable. Yes, there are reports out of science that we may some day conquer death. One vision has nanobots coursing through our bodies and repairing whatever is wrong or diseased. Another report is that scientists at the Geron Corporation and the University of Colorado at Boulder have discovered the "immortality gene," which allegedly controls the aging process in us. The project is to find a way to tell the gene to stop aging the body. But until that day comes, we face death's inevitability.

We have all seen a loved one die. We have seen that last breath, and then they are gone forever—behind a curtain that we cannot penetrate. We have seen and felt their hard, lifeless corpse. We have invented rituals to get us through these moments, but in the end, the coffin is lowered in the earth, and we have to walk away leaving nature to disintegrate their bodies.

Yes, death is difficult for us, and we all know that, barring some miracle, our day will come also. Some in science hold out the possibility that it will some day conquer the last frontier. If it does, that will raise major problems. For example, that would really bankrupt Social Security in the U.S!

Is there life after death in some form? Will we ever see a loved one again?

We do not know when humans got the idea that there was some form of life after death. Does it go back to the very first days of humanity? We may never know. We know that some Chinese used to include food etc. along with a body around 190,000 B.C. The Egyptians, of course, developed their ideas fairly early on as well. All across Africa, China, Vietnam, Europe and so on, there was ancestor worship—in most case, embodying the belief that their ancestors still existed.

What produced such thoughts? Animals do not seem to venerate their ancestors – except maybe elephants, though the evidence on this so far is sketchy. What was it in humans that led them to have such thoughts? Is it a sign of mental weakness—an inability to come to grips with the reality that death is the end, final? Or is it something more?

Sometimes, we have a certain belief about the psychology of our ancestors—that somehow, they did not fully live in the present, that they were escapist, not realists. The fact, of course, is that we do not have anywhere close to a full understanding of their psychology. At times, our attitude towards them is one of superiority—that they were inferior mentally to us. Is this accurate?

It is hard to answer these questions, because we simply do not know. We may gain some clues from our anthropological findings, but the truth is that their state of mind by and large lies behind a curtain that we cannot penetrate.

On the other hand, there is evidence that they had keen minds. Both in Africa in their origins and as they spread across thousands of miles, they had to be realists to survive. They had to think, and think hard. And maybe, just maybe, that hard thinking led them to the conclusion that there was some form of life after death.

What could have possibly led them to this audacious conclusion?

One possible answer is their reflection on the reality of being a human. They obviously saw human beings of many different types and stripes. But they saw in others and felt in themselves an ethical dimension—a wondering about what is right and wrong—and they did not see this in animals. Did this cause them to make the bold, intellectual leap that there was something in humans that was not simply physical—something that could possibly survive the disintegration of the body?

We may never know the answer to this question, but it should give us pause in our own reflections on the reality of death. Our materialist culture quickly reaches the conclusion that there is no life after death. Maybe it is right, but we do not know, and there are reasons why it maybe right to be somewhat skeptical about the materialist's belief.

There is something about a human being that, so far, physics, chemistry, biology and other sciences have not provided an answer to. Maybe one day they will, and then the debate will be over. But maybe that day will never come because maybe it never can.

Why?

Because, rightfully or wrongly, we have, at least at times, a sense that we are not just creatures of flesh and blood and bones, that there is another dimension to us that cannot be reduced to those very earthly things. Some might say that this experience is a sort of mirage produced by certain physical states within us—analogous to when a kettle of water boils and turns to steam. Of course, this analogy limps because steam is still a physical thing.

Maybe those scientists and thinkers who make this claim are right, but prima facie, it is not clear that physical states can produce the experience, for example, of being ethical, because protons and neutrons and electrons and quarks do not possess this property.

If that is so, then we cannot shut the door on this question. The best we can do is to leave it ajar—and that in and of itself is a significant step.

But there is a related and further consideration.

We think that each human being possesses an intrinsic dignity that should not be violated. We do not give the death penalty, for example, to somebody who has killed a dog. Whatever the merits or demerits of the death penalty for killing a human being, nevertheless we make that differentiation between a human and a dog. Is there a profound significance in this difference? It certainly warrants some profound thinking about.

One hard headed realist, Socrates, believed unquestionably that his "psuche"—his conscious thinking self—continued to exist after he died, and he drank the fatal hemlock with a serene cheerfulness, as if this was but one further step on the onward journey of his spirit. How many of us could do that today?

Humans, of course, in times past and today have had a multitude of ideas about the afterlife. Some envisioned it as a glorious paradise, free of earthly suffering, where we would meet our loved ones again and bask in eternal sunshine beside sunlit pools. Whatever the merits or demerits of such beliefs, they are further evidence of the sense of hope that has flowed in the veins of humanity. Even if misplaced, it does not seem to cause much damage to humanity.

However, the lack of ultimate hope in the materialist is cause for deeper concern. Yes, there are many good features about a materialist, but the lack of an ultimate hope leaves a desert of despair at the very roots of the materialist conception of life.

If one were to gamble on this issue—much like Pascal's famous wager to the gamblers in the casinos of Paris—it might be safer to gamble that death is not the total end of a life. If it is the end, we have nothing much to lose. If it is not the end, materialism infects our lives with a false belief that could have deleterious consequences here on earth. It means that all humans do not possess an intrinsic dignity, and the lack of that belief can lead to all sorts of atrocities—slavery, conquest, oppression, gas chambers, etc. The belief that all humans do possess an intrinsic dignity puts a brake on any tendency to engage in such nefarious activities. In our day and age when so many atrocities have been committed by man against his fellow man, we have a need for every belief that would prevent and inhibit such atrocities.

Death, of course, is not an abstract, impersonal topic for all of us. It is not a math problem. It is something intensely personal. That is all the more reason for us to think about it—both in terms of its ultimate implications, and the implications for life here on earth.

It raises for us one of those ultimate questions—who are we?—and how do we determine who we are? In times past, the general answer was that we are more than a physical entity—whether it was called a non-physical entity, a soul, or something else. Today, much of the received wisdom of our scientific age is that we are simply a collection of molecules, atoms and a host of subatomic particles.

Of course, if the former is true, it does not mean that there is life after death. The soul could cease to exist when the body ceases to exist. But, it at least leaves open the possibility of some form of life after death. If there is some form of life, we do not know what form it takes and whether we would be conscious of it in a way that is somewhat analogous to our experience now. If there is no life after death, then obviously we will never know that.

As argued above, it seems hard to espouse the intrinsic dignity of a human being without simultaneously holding that we are more than physical entities. Otherwise, we would in essence be no different than the soil we walk on, or the concrete block that we use to build a wall. We hardly want to say that those things have an intrinsic dignity.

So, the logical conclusion then must be there might be some life after death. If true, that is awesome in its implications and should give us much food for thought. It is also liberating to our spirit to know that we may be more than subatomic particles. If we are just the latter, it would seem that we are not free, and that we are prisoners of the fundamental laws of physics, and that there is nothing we can do to extricate ourselves from them. Hence, this question of life after death has very significant ramifications for us all.

Will we ever embrace death in the way that Socrates did—with joy and calmness and peace? Countless others in times past have done so. If the day ever comes in our culture when people begin to do this again, it will mark a significant change in our culture.

CHAPTER 12

THE WAY FORWARD

Much more could be written about a vast array of subjects such as literature, music, cell phones, movies etc. But if the reader applies the fundamental analysis of this book, he or she can do the requisite evaluation.

We have a future ahead of us—unless of course we destroy ourselves—and we need to face that future, because there is a momentous choice before us. That choice turns on the question of the nature of reality—ourselves included.

Are we simply material entities—a complex mixture of quarks, leptons, and whatever other particles science will discover? Or are we something more? One can have a long debate about this issue, but a full presentation is beyond the scope of this book. Nevertheless, we need to address it.

To use a simple analogy—are we, for example, essentially the same as a rock? A rock has quarks and leptons, so do we. We maybe more complex, but if materialism is correct, we are essentially the same. If so, there should be no moral difference between hammering a rock and hammering a human being.

But we think there is. For example, we put people in prison for the latter but not the former.

Why?

Because we think that a human being is different from a rock. And that is not because we have a different set of particles than a rock. It is because we think there is something about a human being that is profoundly different. Yes, science will continue to explore the physical basis of a human being, and will provide us with a deeper insight into the physical dimension of who we are. But science will never be able to find the particles that constitute the dignity of a human being. That is a boundary that science can never cross.

Is the dignity of each human being merely a figment of the imagination or one of those truths that stare us in the face, and challenge us in our hearts? I argue and believe that it is the latter. If it is not so, then we can put people in places like Auschwitz, or slash peoples' throats like Genghis Kkan, or inflict humiliation like many empires have done.

The intrinsic dignity of each human being—female, male, black, brown, yellow, white, young, old, rich or poor, ugly or beautiful, intelligent or not—is the bedrock principle on which all human endeavor rests.

This principle has been attacked—sometimes overtly, often covertly—in our materialistic age. This is not to say that the previous culture did not violate the principle. It did—often in terrible ways. But that culture at least had a theoretical basis that allowed the possibility of the principle. A materialistic culture does not and cannot.

All the areas of life into which materialism has seeped need to be restructured and reinvigorated with the notion of spirit—or the non-material. The great advances made in the areas of material development are good. But there has to be a parallel advancement in the area of the spirit. The harmonious fusion of the two—with that of the spirit having primacy—is the goal of mankind.

So, whether it is science, art, education, economics, politics or religion, our task is the same. When from early childhood, children are imbued with this principle, then we have a chance at a decent world. It may be stretching language a little, but we are described as mankind. So let us be kind. This is something that I believe in my heart of hearts, and I hope you do also. If so, let us work together to make a world where love, kindness, justice and true joy flourish for all. I know the mountain before us is very high, but let us begin climbing it.

Let us just do it—together!